One
Week
Loan

THE PRIZEFIGHTERS

THE PRIZEFIGHTERS

AN INTIMATE LOOK AT CHAMPIONS AND CONTENDERS

ARLENE SCHULMAN

Foreword by Budd Schulberg

Virgin

First published in Great Britain in 1995 by
Virgin Books
an imprint of Virgin Publishing Ltd
332 Ladbroke Grove
London W10 5AH

First published in the USA by Lyons & Burford

Design by Cindy LaBreacht

A catalogue record of this book is available
from the British Library

ISBN 1 85227 575 8

Printed in the U.S.A.

IN MEMORY OF MY FATHER

CONTENTS

Acknowledgments

WITHOUT THE cooperation of champions and contenders, amateurs and professionals, managers and trainers, gym owners, and others, this book would not have been made possible. Thank you.

In grateful acknowledgment of their assistance and support, advice and encouragement, a round of thanks, from A to Z, to Susan Adams, Howie Albert, Neil Amdur, Stephanie Arcel, Teddy Atlas, Deni Auclair, Phil Berger, Bill Brink, Ed Brophy, Eric Bruskin, Bruce Burris, Víctor Calderón, John Caluwaert, Helene Carter, Tamesha Cley, Nigel Collins, Artemio and María Colón, Linda and Junior Colón, Cathy Colón, Tom Cosentino, Thomas Csiha of Aurora Photo Labs, Bob Decker, Peggy Dickerson, Patti Dreifuss, Don Dunphy, Steve Farhood, Raúl Fernández, Eve Fleisher, Nancy Foote, Jacqui Frazier-Lyde, Marvis Frazier, Ron Fried, Eddie Futch, Bill Gallo, Al Gavin, Mark George, Mary George, Michael George, Patsy Giovanelli, Jimmy Glenn, Bobby Goodman, Murray Goodman, Steve Griffith, Eric Handler, Bill Heinz, Peter Heller, Mauricio Herrador, Dan and Sue Hirshberg, Andy Hsiao, Donna Hughes, Jerry Izenberg, Sandy Jacobs, Anthony James, Judith Janus, Dr. Barry Jordan, Danny Kapilow, Mike Katz, Frank Kelly, Tom Kenville, Dick Klayman, Jeff Klein, Lorraine Kreahling, Leonard Lewin, Butch Lewis, Will Lieberson, Bob Lipsyte, Steve Lott, Tom McGovern, M. J. McKeon, Phil Marder, Darcy Maccarone, Ed Marks, Elizabeth Marlowe, Frank Martínez, Eugene Merinov, Judy Miceli,

Reena Moore, Carl Moretti, Marilyn Munder, LeRoy Neiman, Jack Newfield, Michael Olajide, Sr., Anthony Carter Paige, Robynn Pease, Renita Ragan, Tino Raino, Harry Rhodes, Sylvia Rodríguez, Irving Rudd, Nathan Schulman, Sophie and Martin Schulman, Karen Sellers, Bruce Silverglade, Paul Steele, Aja Zanova Steindler, Emanuel Steward, Steve Stuart, John Szoke, Mark Unthank, Florentina Vasile, Joe Vecchione, Eric Velez, Burt Watson, Allen Wilson, and Vic Zimet.

And in memory of Ray Arcel, Ira Becker, John F. X. Condon, Mike Jones, Marvin Kohn, Barney Nagler, and Manuel de Dios Unanue.

F O R E W O R D
BY BUDD SCHULBERG

I HAVE SEEN Mexican Indians cover their faces when a photographer approaches because they believe the camera will steal their souls.

The photographs of prizefighters taken by Arlene Schulman confirm the ability of the camera, in her gifted hands, to penetrate surfaces to reveal the human truths concealed deeply within.

What I had not anticipated, quite frankly, was a text so finely etched, so intuitively observed, so true to its demanding subject that it becomes all of a piece with its haunting photographs. Text and picture resonate here to bring you closer to the world of prizefighters—that "unpredictable assortment"— than you have ever been before.

It is a world I grew up in, going to the fights twice a week from the age of twelve with my father, knowing champions, contenders, and the "opponents" who sacrifice their bodies and their hearts to the most intense one-on-one contest in all the sports world, the most naked, most cruel and, ironically, most human.

Over the years I've collected fifteen shelves of books on boxing. Homer brings to life an epic contest, and there was Pierce Egan for the English bare-knuckles, and William Hazlitt and Conan Doyle. The special mystique of the ring has caught the attention of American writers generation after generation,

FIGHTER—
Atlanta, Georgia

from Jack London to Ring Lardner, Ernest Hemingway, Nelson Algren, Norman Mailer, Joyce Carol Oates, and others.

I have a special place on my shelf for a novel by Bill Heinz called *The Professional*. He brought you not only into the ring but into the pressure-cooker life outside the ring where, month after month, the boxer endures the sacrifices that will finally bring him to the one critical night that can change his life.

I have seen young boxers who are 20 and 0, who think they are unbeatable, and dream their golden dreams of limos, mansions, and lifetime adulation, the immortality of a Robinson, Louis, or Ali—suddenly cut down to the hard canvas of reality by a perfectly timed right hand to the jaw. I have seen fighters weep in their dressing rooms, not from pain but from that heavy dose of reality that comes with the realization that as good as you think you were, you have now been exposed, reduced to being merely human in this largely misunderstood contest in which not only does body go against body, but mind against mind and will against will.

Reading Arlene Schulman's clear, clean, focused prose, one sees immediately that she knows that mind and has probed that will to provide a composite picture of *The Prizefighters* from top to bottom. She has gone out of her way to interview the champions—Larry Holmes, who goes lumbering on in the ring today although owning a profitable chunk of hometown Easton, Pennsylvania; Roberto Durán, the crafty ex-lightweight, ex-welterweight champion still duking it out with the middleweights when most boxers his age are ten-years retired; and Azumah Nelson, the durable super-featherweight champion from Ghana, whom she goes all the way to visit there. She finds him living and being treated like a king, one of the rare practitioners of this sometimes-sweet science who has mastered both his craft and his life.

But Arlene Schulman knows that for every Nelson there are a thousand—or ten thousand—Don Johnsons, who will never own a Rolls or stretch limo or fill a six-car garage but instead drive a beat-up '75 Camaro, earn purses in the hundreds rather than the millions, and learn the hard lesson early in his career that he'll never be a champion—a blessed Sugar Ray Leonard who started with him in the amateurs—but just "a guinea pig," as his trainer calls him, "... an old timer who hurt his chances when they were using him to bring other people along."

MICHAEL CARBAJAL— World Junior Featherweight Champion

They're all here in this incisive book, the baby hopefuls in the grimy inner-city gyms, and the old champions signing their autographed photos at the Boxing Hall of Fame. As Arlene Schulman explains, despite the stereotype of the brain-damaged pug talking "Dese-dem-dose," there simply are no stereotypes in this complex world. For good reason she closes with Archie Moore, the ten-year light-heavyweight champion who gave a mint-conditioned heavyweight champion Rocky Marciano a hell of a fight when Moore was forty-three, who endured 229 fights against the toughest in his division for almost thirty years and came out of it even more articulate and keen-minded than when he first pulled on a pair of gloves.

If you were scoring this book like a prizefight, you'd have to give Arlene Schulman every round. You don't have to understand or even like boxing to be moved by her humanity, her intuitive "takes" on the personalities of champions and contenders, couldabeens, and wannabes.

INTRODUCTION

I NEVER PUT on a pair of boxing gloves. I never punched a speedbag or heavy bag or an opponent. I have felt smooth leather and worn leather and turned them over in my hands; I have inspected mouthpieces floating in Listerine in mayonnaise jars; I have run my hand over the stitching and the shiny surface of a new satin robe; and I have touched the scarred, sometimes gnarled hands, both firm and soft, of prizefighters. I have listened to their words and observed their faces, and I have wondered why they did what they did.

Their lives—the sacrifice, discipline, preparation, dedication, perspiration, and inspiration, mixed in with a little dream dust—fascinate me. The prizefighter awakens before sunrise to run several miles in the cold and the dark and eats sparingly, mindful of his weight, carefully balancing proteins and carbohydrates. Their bodies pummeled and pounded all day, they retire early to a  chaste bed in a hotel room. They prepare for a fight for a month—maybe three months—away and then see their work succeed or disintegrate in one luminous moment.

Why do they do this?

Boxing is sport and competition, and the community of boxing replaces family, or adds to it. The interests and intelligence of many prizefighters have not been cultivated, so boxing is the only thing they can do. Training six days a week seems much easier than earning a college degree—or even a high-school diploma—and much more honorable than adding figures to a ledger in an office. And the prize—to be the best in the world—is accomplished by only a few.

**FIGHTER—
San Francisco,
California**

An amateur boxing referee introduced me to the sport at the grass-roots level, where it all begins. A film editor, Frank Martínez, and I worked together in the ABC News documentary unit back in the early 1980s. He knew of my interest in photography and invited me to join him one afternoon at a Kid Gloves tournament in front of Madison Square Garden. Founded by John F. X. Condon and run by the Garden, the program (now defunct) ran during the summer months for boys who were ten to fifteen years old and living in New York City or its suburbs. The program provided uniforms and shoes to the boys who boxed in different locations around the city, from the steps of City Hall to the fountains across from the Plaza Hotel, to the Lower East Side and Coney Island. Sometimes the gloves were bigger than they were. These young prize-fighters were black, white, Puerto Rican, Dominican, Haitian, Jamaican, Irish, and Italian. When I began, my photographs silently absorbed some of the weave to the fabric of their lives. Then I decided that the photographs needed a voice, and I began to interview and write stories about these young men, about their lives, about tournaments, about victories and defeats. I worked my way gradually from the amateurs to the professionals, and then to champions and former champions. I traveled from San Francisco to Albuquerque, Miami, Chicago, the Dominican Republic, and Ghana in West Africa. Wherever I traveled, either on business or vacation, I stopped in at the local boxing gym. They became as familiar as a McDonald's; I inhaled the fragrance of perspiration and dedication and marveled at the boxers' discipline.

I found that amateurs and young professionals are willing subjects. Unlike cultures whose peoples are afraid that you might remove a part of them when you photograph them, young boxers like to give you something to remember them by. They feel that the camera and the notebook will save a little piece of them and pass it along. It would make them famous, or, at the very least, prove that they exist.

Champions often have better things to do. Some, like Hollywood celebrities, have a manager, press agent, attorney, entourage, and a cellular phone—and still didn't remember (or care about) schedules. They are difficult to reach, undependable about keeping appointments and if they have something

RING—
Ghana, West Africa

else to do, well, they go and do it. When it comes to photographs, if you click once, they walk away—one photograph should be enough. Sometimes a little bit of coaxing, explaining, or even outright demanding persuaded them to stay a little longer. But not much. And the eagerness and expressiveness of the novice was always gone from their faces. Unlike the face of Muhammad Ali, which is masklike due to his illness, their faces are sculpted by attitude and wariness.

But the prizefighters who used to be champions in a world that no longer exists for them were the most gracious.

Like George Plimpton, I, too, was defeated at the hands of Archie Moore. At eighty or so, he lightly threatens to make a comeback; if he were ten years younger, he probably would. Rather than test my skills against him in the ring, I took my chances at pool. After valiant efforts to interrupt his concentration, I began swiping the balls that he had just shot into the pockets out of the pockets and putting them back onto the table when he wasn't looking. He would interrupt his shots long enough to change jazz records on his record player. I moved balls for a more accurate shot and pushed them into pockets when he turned away. Still, he beat me resoundingly.

Like myself, Moore is an inveterate thrift-shop shopper. Neither of us necessarily needs anything, but there's the thrill of finding someone else's castaways or an antique or two, and searching through dusty bins for a hard-to-find book, an old record album, or clothing. One week, Moore's daughter said, he came home with five record players—and she had presented him with a new stereo for Christmas. Once when he went out of town, his family rented a Dumpster and cleaned out some of the junk that he had accumulated. He beat me here, too. But only by a split decision.

Over the time that I traveled to photograph and interview fighters, I managed to turn up at almost every Salvation Army and thrift shop in the city or town that I visited. I trooped through some of the country's best hotels toting a typewriter, a sewing machine, a Joe Louis clock, a Sugar Ray Robinson hand puppet, an art deco wall clock, two teapots (I don't drink tea), a coffeepot (I don't drink coffee), an accordion (I don't play), two cups sculpted in wire, an old Brownie camera, a too-large kimono, a pocketbook, an antique one-sided photographer's chair, two old kitchen whisks, and a few other items too undistinguished to remember. What I saw in the thrift shops told me what kind of town I was in.

Erie, Pennsylvania, where Roberto Durán trained, was dismal and dank, and colorless. I circled the downtown area a few times before accidentally bumping into it. The local thrift shop was crowded with cheap castaways: badly made clothing hanging limply on hangers, frayed bedspreads and incomplete games, stained workshirts for sale and used men's underwear showcased on skirt hangers. Durán was not interested in bargains—only training—and there were no diversions for him in Erie. Or for me.

Houston, where Evander Holyfield and Thomas Hearns were training, had the most thrift shops, with clothes arranged neatly, in wide aisles; if you chose, you could outfit yourself in a surgeon's scrub suit and mink stole. San Diego—Moore's hometown—had the most shops within a three-block radius

(there were four), and I looked for bargains next to Mexicans who had no other choice but to shop at places where Navy veterans and their wives shipped their no-longer-wanted items. Theirs must have been a transient life. There were occasional evening dresses, a tux or two, but no sign of the bric-a-brac that one accumulates over time. Minneapolis stocked polyester leisure suits; Chicago, old typewriters, crutches, and skis. In every town, I found a wild assortment of orphaned pots without lids and lids without pots.

The men who chose to become prizefighters or who discovered that it was their calling are just as unpredictable an assortment—from the illiterate (John Tate) to the literate (José Torres), from the preachers (George Foreman and Earnie Shavers) to those in need of salvation (Tony Ayala), from the gregarious (Ray Mancini) to the solemn (Thomas Hearns), from the revered (Muhammad Ali) to the fallen (Leon Spinks).

They have their own sense of time. Prizefighters are trained to respond only when the bell rings. As the subject of an interview, in spite of a Rolex, a stopwatch, and an entourage, 3:00 could mean anything from 4:00 to 5:00 and then 6:00 and well, maybe the next day. Rarely was it 3:00. I tried to think the way they did, so I showed up twenty minutes late one day, figuring that I would have to wait anyway. Junior Jones showed up fifteen minutes early. So I arrived on time no matter what and came prepared with a newspaper or magazine. It wasn't personal. These men were meant to fight, not to keep appointments.

I took Leon Spinks to lunch, and when he excused himself from the table before we even had a chance to order, I wondered whether he would return. (He did.) Julio César Chávez has someone ring the elevator for him so that he doesn't have to wait—but he kept me waiting for a day in Tijuana, Mexico. When José Torres worked for the Dinkins campaign, he invited me to join him and his colleagues in a campaign van. They were to meet with then-New York City Mayor David Dinkins as he spoke at a hospital in Elmhurst, Queens. Attempting to make a U-turn in traffic in the pouring rain, Torres was hit on the left side by a tank of a car. His wife sighed, and he scrambled out to inspect the damage. It was his first accident in thirty years, he announced, sounding disappointed. He exchanged licenses with the angry driver, placating him with "Are you related to —?," some name that I've since forgotten, adding, "He was one of my early opponents." The driver seemed impressed. His car was barely scratched. Torres and company drove off in the rain searching for Elmhurst and Torres arrived just in time to pose for photographs with the Mayor.

Michael Spinks talked for so long (four hours) in Butch Lewis's office that Lewis was dumbfounded. Almost in tears, Spinks spoke of the frustration he felt when he dealt with his older brother, Leon, and his nervousness at raising his teen-aged daughter alone. Montell Griffin ironed his sweatpants and changed his clothes because the crease wasn't right. Mark Breland, who works out harder now than he did when he was fighting, still has a waist so small that it seems you could wrap your hands around it. His car was in the shop and

he worried whether taxis would stop for him—a black man, a former champion—as he waited on Second Avenue.

I met honest men and schemers, the well-to-do and the down-and-out, the intelligent and the unintelligible, the meek and mild who assumed another identity when they donned a robe and trunks, ex-cons and con artists, family men and lechers, religious men and sinners, friends and foes, the descriptive and the nondescript, the fastidious and the lazy, the cruel and the sensitive, the doomed and the dead.

I could have interviewed and photographed a thousand men.

But I chose to narrate a sampling of the lives of some who became prizefighters. One man's story, told well, can be infinitely more fascinating than bits and pieces of many. If anyone is left out, it is not because of their genius and talent in the boxing ring. Jack Sharkey and Tony Zale are both in nursing homes; their families prefer to have them remembered as they once were. Several, including Mike Tyson and Sugar Ray Leonard, did not respond to my requests for interviews, or were not available.

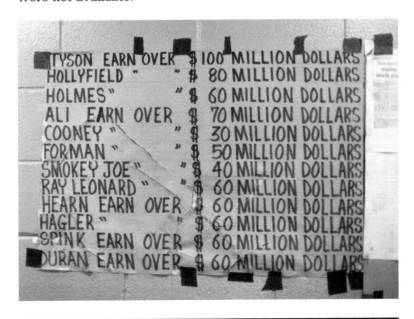

The glimpses of these fighters caught through my camera and through my interviews represents only the short time that we were together and only a small part of them.

Prizefighters enter the ring alone and they leave alone, their years of training and perspiration tested in the moment that it takes a gloved fist to travel a dozen inches. There are unknown kids with a dream blazing in their heads and men who have won world championships and millions of dollars. Then, they, too, are replaced by someone younger, faster, stronger, and the cycle begins again; they retire and make comebacks until they are finally content that they are no longer young. I chose to document these men not only as a historical record, but also to illustrate, as Archie Moore says, that a fighter is not filled with "dem," "dat," or "dose." None of them was.

Some boxing gyms, like Gleason's, have relocated. Others, like New York City's Times Square Gym and Gramercy Gym and Miami's Fifth Street Gym, have closed up and then been torn down. They weren't quite museums; but if you look closely in the shadows, you can see the ghosts of old champions and contenders who worked out there. The grit and grime and smells  of these old places no longer exist; their history is gone, too.

I hope that you find in *The Prizefighters* an intimate and revealing look at champions and contenders, and the world in which they live.

Arlene Schulman
New York City
June 1994

G · Y · M · S

THE WESTSIDE Athletic Club in New York City's Washington Heights doesn't show up on any maps or in any guidebooks listing health-and-fitness clubs; signs and arrows are nonexistent, and sometimes it takes the neighbors a few minutes to remember that it's there. "Oh, yes, it's Colón's place around the corner," they reply in Spanish. Make a left past bins of vegetables and men lounging outside the corner bodega, past women carrying groceries and children, and walk

Westside Athletic Club

around young men vacuuming the inside of their red-velvet sedans across from a dog lapping at a dripping fire hydrant and skinny girls wearing pale summer dresses under too-short winter coats and neighbors peeking from behind curtains and then make a sharp right turn in the middle of the block. Inch down a flight of crooked stairs, where chips of broken-off cement make triangular patterns in the sun, and step lightly over stinking, rotting garbage piled precariously in overfilled tin garbage cans in the narrow unlit tunnel that leads toward a landscape blooming with decaying artifacts of last night's dinner that neighbors so flippantly tossed out of their windows. Push open a door, complete with doorbell and peephole, tentatively, and as you peek into the dinginess, the sound of gloves beating leather and the fast heartbeat of the speedbag is unmistakable.

Welcome to the Westside Athletic Club and gym bags full of dreams, lockers full of hope, and flurries of furious hands— and a gentle man with a life full of disappointments, disasters, and promises who clings to his dream. In the thirty-five years that he has run the gym, Artemio Colón has never had a professional championship fighter. That is his dream.

With his triangular-shaped fingerprint-smudged glasses, thick, shiny black hair, and diminutive frame, Colón looks like a wizened elf. He opened the gym in 1959 with just a weight room, and by 1963, a boxing ring, speedbags, and heavy leather punching bags had been added. Six inches off the floor, the ring is covered by a grimy well-traveled canvas and lit by a single lightbulb. Showers, a single toilet, lockers, and a refrigerator are in the back. Tables are covered with gloves, headgear, and jump ropes, the windows with bars. The rocky walls, painted a chalky white, boast a decorator's touch of black-and-white photographs in smoky lucite frames, placed at odd intervals. A large black-and-white Rocky Marciano photo in a cracked frame, a corkboard with announcements, and a handprinted sign imploring that gym clothes be washed complete the rest of the decor.

The boys and young men that he has taught to box never had posters stapled to lampposts outside of Madison Square Garden or hanging in lobbies of casinos, never earned enough to make a living from boxing, and never got close enough to

ROCKY MARCIANO

put fingerprints on Colón's dream. These were the understudies: the men who fought in tiny shows in smaller towns like some second-rate touring company. But they kept auditioning. Some were just not good enough; others had the talent, but could never combine that duet of talent and steely desire. Still others trained simply for exercise, but arrived more regularly than those who trained for a fight the following week, and others were just passing time. Some fooled themselves, but they never fooled him. They were black, Hispanic, Asian, and white. Some were young and some were too old. Some spoke English; most didn't. He taught them to jab, to hook, to bob and weave. He held their ankles as they struggled through sit-ups, and he held their heads in his hands as he wiped off sweat, Vaseline, and tears with a white towel. They learned how to win and how to live with defeat.

Some took advantage of Colón's kindness. If they couldn't afford gym dues, he let it pass; and when they disappeared

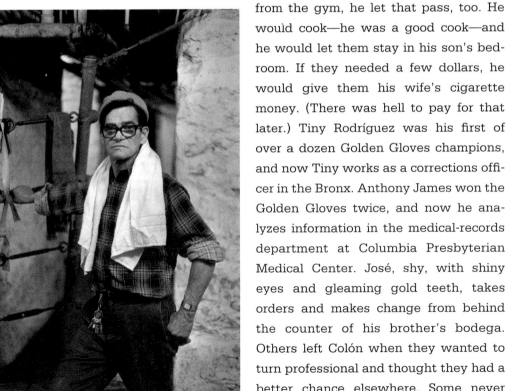

ARTEMIO COLÓN

from the gym, he let that pass, too. He would cook—he was a good cook—and he would let them stay in his son's bedroom. If they needed a few dollars, he would give them his wife's cigarette money. (There was hell to pay for that later.) Tiny Rodríguez was his first of over a dozen Golden Gloves champions, and now Tiny works as a corrections officer in the Bronx. Anthony James won the Golden Gloves twice, and now he analyzes information in the medical-records department at Columbia Presbyterian Medical Center. José, shy, with shiny eyes and gleaming gold teeth, takes orders and makes change from behind the counter of his brother's bodega. Others left Colón when they wanted to turn professional and thought they had a better chance elsewhere. Some never had any. David had a newborn son and a drug habit to support. He turned up at Riker's periodically, and when he was released, he would turn up at Colón's. And then he never showed up again. Someone saw him sleeping in the back of a bus heading uptown, his destination unknown. But Colón has never been interested in destinations—only journeys, and if journeys ended after one or two or three fights, well, then that was okay, too.

You can find a Westside Athletic Club from Albuquerque to Detroit to Washington, D.C., to San Francisco to Miami, in broken-down urban areas, in basements, second floors, youth centers, recreation centers, Police Athletic Leagues, old warehouses, and apartment buildings.  Tommy Morrison, who once held a heavyweight title, trained on the front porch of his home in Oklahoma with a heavy bag made out of a duffel bag filled with old clothes. Men and boys who decide that they, too, must become Heavyweight Champion of the World arrive at the gym. Other show up as children, imitating their fathers or friends, too small even to move the heavy bag. A few come from prison, and some come from the streets—reformed drug users preaching the fire and brimstone of their new lives. Fighters walked up the creaking, lopsided stairs to reach the Gramercy Gym on 14th Street in New York City, where Cus D'Amato trained Floyd Patterson and José Torres before he moved to the Catskills to train Mike Tyson. "It looked like you were going all the way up to heaven," D'Amato once said.

The gyms have their own unique wallpaper of fight posters, newspaper clippings, photographs, and handwritten signs written in Magic Marker designed to inspire or remind: *Notice: Please all visitors must try not to discuss their opinions during training hours. Thank you!* or *Pay Your Dues! Don't Be Average. Winners Don't Quit.* Some gyms are larger, more productive and profitable, like Detroit's Kronk Gym; and some are smaller, like the Westside Athletic Club. Some produced world champions, most haven't. But the smell of ancient sweat is the same. Many gyms have closed over the last ten years; rents increased and attendance dwindled. "The talent

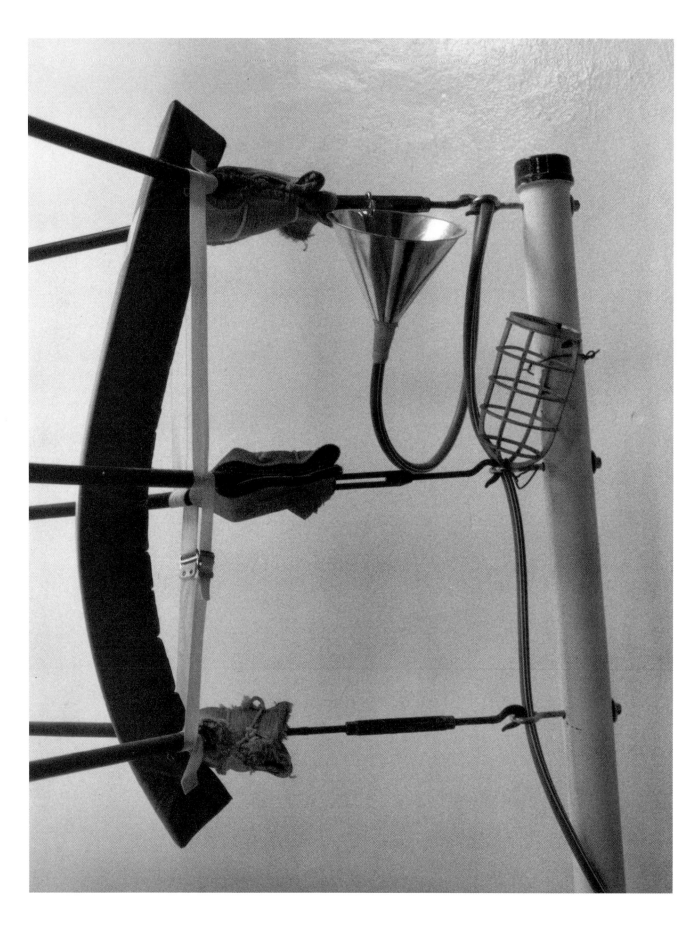

started drying up because drugs started getting to many of the kids," trainer George Benton says, sounding defeated.

For the men who tiptoe in at 65 pounds or tiptoe out at 265 pounds, the rules are similar: No drugs, no drinking, respect women, watch what you eat, go to bed early, get up at six for roadwork, hit the speedbag and heavy bag, do your sit-ups, shadowbox, lift a few weights, spar a few rounds. Every day except Sunday. Like Colón, their trainers hold a stopwatch, water bottle, the towel, a jar of Vaseline. They serve as chauffeur, cook, secretary, manager. Sometimes a hot plate or a fast-food restaurant has to do for out-of-town bouts where no one in the crowd roots for them. Shorts and a robe, if there is one, are not custom made, some are dingy, or too large or too

small. With most higher-ranking contenders and the champions—the stars—the routine is almost the same, except that they set up impromptu training camps at posh hotels, casinos, and resorts and order from room service. The rooms are cleaner, the prizes larger. Emanuel Steward caters to his fighters, especially Thomas Hearns and, for a short time, Evander Holyfield; he cooks separate meals daily for each fighter in his camp. "Tommy and Evander are strictly home-cooking guys who like stewed chicken and baked beans," he confides. "Evander doesn't like nothing cooked from the can and nothing frozen. Everything must be fresh. I know what they like. Tommy doesn't eat pork. Gerald McClellan (a WBC middleweight champion) does not eat chicken. He eats liver and rice. And he only want me to cook it. Sometimes,"—he sighs— "he wants pancakes for dinner."

Riddick Bowe asks a friend to pick up Kentucky Fried Chicken. The heavyweight champion also has a young friend to hand him a towel before he needs it. Another clocks his sprints along the beach; another gives him a relaxing massage. Someone else answers the phone. Thomas Hearns has

The Spitting Cup

**RIDDICK BOWE,
EDDIE FUTCH—
Lake Tahoe, Nevada**

Emanuel Steward as his manager and trainer, but he also has his brother as chief cheerleader and towel man. Another man, video camera in hand, videotapes the sparring sessions and serves as a driver and gofer. Hearns travels with a bodyguard "just in case." Evander Holyfield has a strength-and-conditioning coach who puts him through a scientific range of weights and exercises, a ballet teacher, and a suitcase full of vitamins. Larry Holmes built his own gym.

"We kind of bridge the gap between the old method and the new," say trainer Thell Torrence, a disciple of Eddie Futch who has trained the heavyweight champions Ken Norton, Joe Frazier, Michael Spinks, and Riddick Bowe. "A lot of young trainers don't know anything. We used to take the guy into the woods, get him an ax, and have him hack on stumps. Then we would find him a sledgehammer. They don't do that anymore, but the end result is the same. The Olympic training camp has had some benefits," he admits. "It's now all very scientific, like checking the cardiovascular rate. But we used to do that from instinct, like the old aviators. You know how hard to push your fighter. You would increase running, pick up the tempo, slow it down. You can look at the fighter and tell how to get the maximum effort from your product. You didn't need all these people."

Stillman's Gym hosted an encyclopedia of champions, contenders, characters, sparring partners, trainers, mobsters, and gamblers before Lou Stillman retired in 1959. Ray Arcel, Freddie Brown, Whitey Bimstein, and Al Silvani trained fighters for eight hours a day, and then some. Angelo Dundee, just out of the Army, slept on a cot and carried buckets and bags and learned. A great trainer is a natural: he actually sees the moves and studies them, and he must have the ability to convey techniques to his fighters. He must be a psychologist and

a mind reader, sometimes a father and a mother. Now, compared to the teamwork of Steward and Hearns and, earlier, Arcel with any of his fighters, Larry Holmes and George Foreman tell their trainers what to do.

Training Camp, Héctor Camacho

In 1935, Stillman's opened at 55th and Eighth Avenue, after moving from 125th Street in Harlem. Sometimes as many as 200 spectators would watch a fabled list of fighters train, from Lou Ambers, Joe Louis, Rocky Graziano, Kid Gavilán, Beau

GEORGE BENTON—
Trainer

Jack, Sandy Saddler, Benny Leonard, Rocky Marciano, and Joey Maxim. Sparring was fierce, with first- and second-ranked contenders matched against each other. Main-event fighters were often plucked from the crowd and given top billing at Madison Square Garden on the next evening's fight card. Jack Johnson and Jack Dempsey would watch from the sidelines.

Bobby Gleason, who used to drive a cab, opened his gym one flight up on Westchester Avenue in the Bronx in 1937. Dues were just two dollars a month when Jack LaMotta and Phil Terranova trained there. Gleason's moved to 30th Street and Eighth Avenue in 1975, just a few blocks from Madison Square Garden, where workers from the fur and garment districts would pay a dollar for admission and stop over on their lunch hour to watch Emile Griffith bantering with several of the boxers he trained or Eusebio Pedroza skipping rope in a corner. Gerry Cooney, Roberto Durán, Vito Antuofermo, Saoul Mamby, Héctor Camacho, Livingston Bramble, Larry Holmes, and Michael Spinks trained alongside amateurs and contenders. More than eighty-five world champions trained at Gleason's. The place was small: two tightly packed rings against one wall, and heavy bags and speedbags in the dimly lit back areas. The boxers dressed downstairs. Special dressing rooms upstairs were reserved for a local contender or world-champion-in-training. Movies and commercials were

filmed there, and it was a gathering place for writers. Gleason's moved once more, this time to Brooklyn in 1987 when their lease expired, and the rent was raised. It was rumored that the old Gleason's would be converted into condominiums, but a company that sells packing boxes took over the space. They left the marine-blue paint on the walls and the Gleason's Gym sign that hangs from the second-floor balcony.

At Miami's Fifth Street Gym, Angelo Dundee tried to keep Willie Pastrano in shape, Muhammad Ali entertained Howard Cosell and other reporters, and Beau Jack, rescued from a job shining shoes, presided over fighters' constitutions from an office plastered with photographs. The gym was torn down in 1993 and replaced by a parking lot.

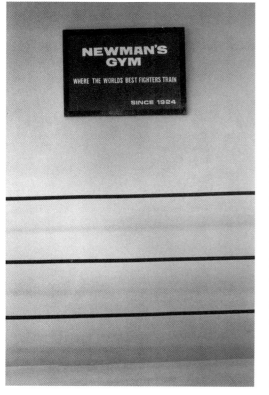

The parking lot in front of the Kronk Gym was empty before Thomas Hearns became a champion. Bus schedules were pasted on the walls, and Hearns would check for his bus and run for it. After he became champion, the parking lot became a symbol of success. Hearns parks his Rolls-Royce next to the Rolls-Royce owned by Emanuel Steward. And when Evander Holyfield trained at the Kronk Gym, he parked his limo out front.

Using the ring as his mattress and a towel as a pillow, World Champion Emile Griffith slept in the ring at the Times Square Gym under the stinking, sweaty perfume of champions and contenders. The gym was airless in the summer and overheated during the winter, and the sound of buses, taxis, and noisy arguments would rise to the

The Weight

second-floor gym and disturb his sleep. Streetlights threw shadows across fight posters papered from floor to ceiling and, resting from their hours of furious beatings, the heavy bags were finally still. The rotting wood floor creaked as Griffith tiptoed to his bed; passing a panel of mirrors, his reflection splintered into pieces by a starburst of cracks. Muhammad Ali glared at him from one wall; Don King, Ken Norton, and Roberto Durán from another. Beaten and broken chairs formed a necklace around his mattress of soiled can-

vas held together with peeling tape. The ceiling sagged, its
floor creaked, the moldy shower stank, wallets and jackets
occasionally turned up missing, and once someone dropped a
gun that went off in the third-floor locker room, the bullet
tearing through the floor and barely missing someone skipping rope. Not very many people noticed. Girlie photos were
pasted on a couple of lockers and formed a collage along the
walls of one closet. A large green feathery plant which someone must have watered stood next to the large plate-glass

window that read "Times Square Gym" backward as you looked out onto 42nd Street.

The Times Square Gym stank of damp leather, lockers stuffed with forgotten, sweaty clothes, and perspiration that stuffed your nose and clung to your clothes. It was the last gym in New York City to have that fertile smell. Gleason's Gym had it, but Gleason's commercialized the sport—perhaps not a bad strategy in an economic pinch. Wall Street executives train alongside women who share a speedbag with a Golden Gloves champion sparring with a writer pretending to be George

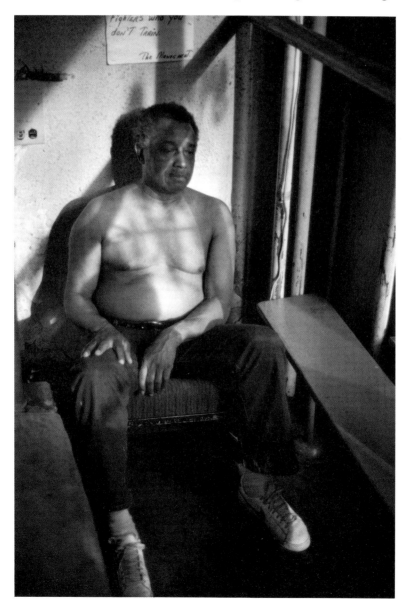

**EDWIN ROSARIO—
Lightweight
Champion, Times
Square Gym (left)**

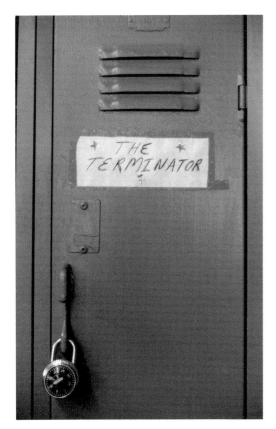

Plimpton pretending to be a boxer. The Times Square Gym, in all its decay, tried hard not to compromise, not to pretend to be more than it was. The Times Square Gym was a place where a kid learned how to make a fist, where trainers would push, cajole, and despair over their fighters, where managers would search for their golden boy, where prizefighters waited outside for the door to open and where fighters were told that they didn't have it anymore. Champions trained alongside novices who whispered, "That's Roberto Durán." Durán always drew the biggest crowd.

"It was so much fun then," Griffith recalled. "I used to love to train there. If this place could speak, man"—he bowed his head—"it was wonderful to us."

An American flag hangs from a clothesline next to patched punching bags in this grimy theater of dreams. The gym was standing—but wearily—until the fall of 1993. Griffith, who trains fighters for a living these days, had moved to Gleason's the year before. All of the champions and most of the old men had left in the months before it closed. A few contenders lingered under the aroma of better days. And then they, too, were gone.

Standing squarely in the middle of the area of Times Square slated for demolition, the block where the Times Square Gym stands will be wiped clean, and a sparkling fifty-seven-story office tower will replace the three-story building where the narrow stairs leaned to the left.

"Well," Griffith said, as he sat on a long narrow bench next to the plant, absentmindedly touching its leaves, "I never dreamed that it was going to go down—I never thought that they would tear down this building. We took it for granted. I feel sad. This is like home."

ALCHOLIC BEVERAGES
are
NOT PERMITTED
ON THESE PREMICES
AT ANY TIME.

THE MANAGEMENT
— TIMES SQUARE A.C. —

NOTICE

NO PERSON MAY COMMUNICATE
TH A FIGHTER ENGAGED IN A
RRING SESSION, UNLESS SUCH
SON IS A TRAINER OR MANAGER
ICH FIGHTER!

IS RULE SHALL BE STRICTLY
NFORCED.

The MANAGEMENT

"It was only a matter of time," said Jimmy Glenn, the gym's owner, in 1993. "We had been here for sixteen years. I knew it was going to happen. They're trying to clean up Forty-Second Street," he said, wrapping a rag around his hand and wiping a stain from the glass-topped counter of his bar—Jimmy's Corner, two blocks over and around the corner from the gym. "I remember everything . . . all the kids . . . you remember the kids that didn't make it in boxing. Someone taught them respect and put them in the right direction.

"I'll cry . . . that's life." He shrugged. "We'll take all the posters and the ring and the lockers—and the plant."

Griffith at least hopes to get a memento. "I hope that when they take it down, I can get a nice brick. I have a brick from the old Madison Square Garden. I'm going to pass by when it's torn down and try to hear some noise from upstairs," he said of the Times Square Gym.

At the Westside Athletic Club, Colón keeps hoping for someone like Hearns or Holyfield, Griffith or Marciano. Every so often, a new face travels to the gym, past the men and the garbage and the women and children, and the seventy-five-year-old Colón takes down a pair of worn gloves from the nail in the wall again. He asks, "Do you think I'll have a world champion before I die?"

The Professionals, Times Square Gym

THE PRIZEFIGHTERS

The wolf loses his teeth, but not his inclinations.
—SPANISH PROVERB

329 stitches   11 broken noses
2 broken cheekbones   8 cracked ribs

THE STIGMATA of sixteen years in boxing are retold in the face of Chuck Wepner. From the beginning, he was marked. He fought Sonny Liston—and lost—in Liston's last bout, six months before Liston was mysteriously found dead. That bout gave Wepner seventy-two stitches, a broken nose, and a broken left cheekbone. "These were the kinds of guys that I was fighting," Wepner said without apology. "Why?" he repeated, his eyes searching around his living room filled with plaques and trophies. "Because I liked it."

They were born to become prizefighters and nothing else.

"I was born to fight," said Roberto Durán. "I don't know what else to do."

The best become legends, others legendary; some remain contenders or dilettantes—just a name under someone else's record. Their styles in the ring are as different as their origins and their personalities. To study them is to see portraits of flattened noses and scar tissue, strong necks bearing proud heads, eyes that have seen victory, endured defeat, and, outside the ring, often look gentle, intelligent, whimsical, or tired, eyes that sparkle with humor or are dull with disappointment.

EDDIE DAVIS—
Light Heavyweight
Contender

ANTHONY JAMES—
Golden Gloves
Champion

Features change over time. Evander Holyfield's handsome face has flattened itself out in some spots and become lumpy in others. "Boxing's a rough sport," Muhammad Ali once said. "After every fight I rush to the mirror to make sure I'm still presentable. A lot of boxers' features change," he added, "when I fight 'em." The best physiques—whether large, like Holyfield, or small, like Michael Carbajal—look like sculpture, carved muscles in perfect proportion. And there is an aura about a man who knows that he is the best in the world.

A loud and persuasive voice shouts to them to stick their hands into a pair of sweaty gloves, to learn the basic techniques of boxing, to prove their skills against others, to compete, to win, to get out of the neighborhood, to become a champion. Some fight in the streets, in school, at home, in prison; others hold it inside. Brother may follow brother, like Michael and Leon Spinks, a father may show off rusty skills to his son, like Nick Barbella to Rocky Graziano; and even a mother may instruct her son, like the light heavyweight Egerton Marcus, whose mother learned to box as a teenager in her native Guyana. Sometimes they find their way into the ring by chance.

When Cassius Clay turned twelve, his father bought him a new bicycle for Christmas, and he rode it proudly to a large bazaar in town called "The Louisville Home Show." He left his

EVANDER
HOLYFIELD—
World Heavyweight
Champion

bicycle outside while he went to look around, and when he came outside, it was gone. He was very upset and afraid of what his father would say. Someone sent him to see a policeman named Joe Martin at the Columbia Boxing Gym. When he saw the gym, Cassius Clay almost forgot that his bicycle was missing. Boys were boxing each other and skipping rope, and

The Loser—
Atlanta, Georgia

he could hear the rat-tat-tat of the speedbag and the hard punches to the heavy bag. The air smelled like perspiration and liniment. Joe Martin invited the excited Cassius to join and sent him home with an application.

A few days later, while Cassius was flipping television channels, he noticed Martin coaching amateur boxers on a show called *Tomorrow's Champions*. Cassius decided that he would join Joe Martin's gym. "I want to be a boxer," he told his mother.

"They are all very different human beings," said trainer Angelo Dundee. "They've all come from different beginnings."

Beau Jack, born Sidney Walker in Augusta, Georgia, became upset when neighborhood bullies grabbed his shoe polish. His grandmother insisted that he fight back and, following her instructions, he knocked out the group's leader. Beau Jack became a fighter who threw punches from bell to

Boxer and Son—
Bronx, New York

Rome
Boxing Club
(right)

bell and knocked out Tippy Larkin for the world lightweight title in 1942.

Willie Pastrano, born in New Orleans, wanted only to win a few amateur fights to show off his trophies and medals to his girlfriends. He had no interest in becoming a professional fighter. A careful boxer with good footwork who was more defensive than aggressive, he could knock out an opponent when he had to. He fought for over ten years without a chance to win a title until he won the world light-heavyweight title when he was twenty-eight in his seventy-eighth fight in 1963.

Rocky Graziano, a middleweight champion of the world, was born Thomas Rocco Barbella on Manhattan's Lower East Side and was in and out of reform schools and street fights. Graziano decided to become a boxer to earn an honest living, he said; a decision that saved his life. He was a street fighter in the ring, a brawler, and a tremendous puncher with either hand. Graziano fought twenty times in 1944. He won and lost his title to Tony Zale; he stopped Zale in 1947, and Zale returned the favor less than a year later. Graziano fought twenty-two more times in three-and-a-half years before he had another chance at the title. This time, he was knocked out by Sugar Ray Robinson. He lost once more, and then retired.

Carlos Monzón shined shoes, sold newspapers, and delivered milk in Santa Fé, Argentina. He fought for fourteen years, a complete fighter who could box a fighter and fight a boxer. The world middleweight champion in the 1970s, he won his title in 1970 against Nino Benvenuti, made fourteen title defenses, and then retired, still champion.

Tomás Molinares, a welterweight champion in the late 1980s, used to wake up in the mornings on the mattress he shared with his three brothers and sisters and step onto the dirt floor in Cartagena, Colómbia. He had to carry water in buckets, and there was no electricity. Rain used to leak through the walls and ceilings of his plywood-and-cardboard house, and he had to wade through mud. Sometimes it was like washing your feet, he said. As he tiptoed around his bed and the one shared by his parents in the one-room house, he read the sports pages. Antonio Cervantes was the world junior welterweight champion, and he was always big news. "That got me thinking," Molinares said. "I wanted to get into boxing to help my family."

AARON DAVIS and Son—Welterweight Champion

53

"I can now buy my mama a house made of bricks with a toilet that flushes," said Danilo Cabrera, a featherweight from the Dominican Republic.

Some fighters came from the neighborhoods where, if you lived there long enough, you'd be killed. Riddick Bowe rose from a neighborhood of crack houses in Bedford-Stuyvesant; Roberto Durán slept in the streets of Panama; Larry Holmes shined shoes for a couple of dollars in Easton, Pennsylvania; Mike Tyson fought his way through reform school; Rubin "Hurricane" Carter was imprisoned for twenty years for murders he did not commit; Tony Ayala is still in prison. Some, like Thomas Hearns, dropped out of school—Hearns in the eleventh grade, Larry Holmes in the seventh grade, while Roberto Durán, who never made it past the third grade, improved his reading skills by reading boxing magazines.

Boxing offers discipline and the acclaim of being the best from a neighborhood full of losers; it provides worshippers and handshakers and, with a few calculated fights, a tremendous amount of money. It is a sport where the rewards outweigh the risks, where a man can earn more respect and money in thirty minutes than in thirty lifetimes. Any other form of employment represents routine and drudgery—few accountants and teachers find their names on Las Vegas marquees. Boxers become heroes—to outfielders and quarterbacks, chefs, conductors, stockbrokers and secretaries, postal carriers and presidents; to writers, artists, actors, and musicians, the newly employed and the unemployed; to the young, the middle-aged, and the old. They are revered for their fighting skills, imitated, adored, and reviled. Instead of learning calculus, they learn the proper way to throw a left hook. Instead of discovering the heroes and villains in Shakespeare, they learn how to hit the speedbag.

But there is the stereotype. "I don't know how the stereotype could be changed," said Archie Moore, the world light-heavyweight champion. "Every fighter doesn't use 'dem,' 'dat,' or 'dose.' People get stereotypes from certain movies and ghetto movies where the hero plays the part of the dummy. The publicity people—the writers—would have to change that. They destroy the story and the storyteller. They make him sound like an idiot on TV," he grumbled. "Many have gotten a far better education than those who have gone to college. I've traveled to Africa, to Europe. How better can you learn than by experience?"

"The stereotype of all fighters is that they're dumb," said Buddy McGirt, who has always admired Archie Moore. "The hell with them."

They must have intelligence, and then the instinct to see a punch before it's halfway there, to time a jab perfectly, to map out their strategy, to move out of the way in an instant. Just as each style is unique, boxing is a game made up of individuals.

**ARCHIE MOORE—
World Light-
Heavyweight
Champion**

"I don't have a ten-room mansion," states McGirt, a junior welterweight and welterweight champion from Brentwood, Long Island. A classic-style boxer with minimal moves, he is not flashy, and he fights with even less recognition. "I've got three bedrooms. That's all. I've got six kids, four cars, and a truck. No vacations," he added. "I vacation in Brentwood."

Between fights, Riddick Bowe oversees a $7-million-home with a sixteen-car garage, a waterfall, billiard room, bowling alley, a beauty parlor, and barbershop on Riddick Bowe Court. A physical fighter who is usually the dominant force of the match, he bangs his opponents around before they fall. Sometimes he can be calculating; his responses are carefully thought out. When he decides to retire, he is considering a career—well, some kind of career—in the military. "Going into the military is something that I always wanted to do," he said.

**BUDDY McGIRT—
Junior Welterweight
and Welterweight
Champion**

**RIDDICK BOWE—
World Heavyweight
Champion, Lake
Tahoe, Nevada**

"I would want the experience, and I like the uniform. I don't want to kill. It gives you direction and discipline, and I like the pictures of the guys in their hats and uniforms. Maybe," he added, "I'll just have my picture taken in uniform."

Bowe traveled to Somalia, greeting the troops and writing a large check to be used to feed the hungry. He is from Bedford-Stuyvesant, where the war on drugs and poverty has yet to be won. "I was moved by the kids," he said quietly, staring into a bowl of soup. "They were still able to smile. I felt that a dog shouldn't have to live that way. I wouldn't wish that on anyone. But the kids bothered me. I wanted them to know that not everyone has forgotten them over there," he said. "I was nervous. I took two day trips to Somalia, to the

RIDDICK BOWE—
Brooklyn, New York

war zone. You never know who can turn up dead. One of the nurses was ambushed and killed. But I'm in a position where people would listen. I can use my position to help other people. When my career is over, I hope the majority of people will see me as someone who tried to look out for everybody."

Tommy Morrison, his style unrefined and inconsistent, used his power as a heavyweight to make his own decisions. "When I started making six figures, I felt the need to get more involved. I was the biggest part of the corporation but I had no idea what I was paying for," he explained. "It was kind of depressing what I was finding out. People are not in this business to lose money. I would fight for an $80,000 or $100,000 purse. My manager would give me 67 percent, and then 40 percent went for taxes. There would be a fight for $100,000, and my end would be $22,000. I'm getting nothing," he complained. "I questioned that. I asked, 'What is the manager doing for 33 percent?!' My manager was charging me for postage, a tape of a cassette, for commuting back and forth, for all of these little things. This is part of the percentage. I felt that it was unfair. It was more Bill Cayton than anyone else. Bill handles the fight things. Bill would fly first-class everywhere, John Brown would have me endorse equipment, and then I would be charged for it in camp. Now I get it for free," he declared. "John Brown handles the training, transportation, housing, room and board. Bill handles contracts, fights, and negotiations for purses. I had to go and confront Bill," he said. "People will do whatever you allow them to do. I told him how I thought this should happen: 'Either agree with me or there will be a problem.' I wanted to know what the hell was going on."

Thomas Hearns has more titles than many kings and princes. But this royalty is alone on his thirty-fifth birthday, playing cards with his manager and trainer, Emanuel Steward, in a rented apartment in Houston, where he is in training. His belts—the WBA welterweight, the WBC junior middleweight, WBC middleweight, and WBC and WBA light-heavyweight—are displayed behind glass in his home in Detroit. As quick as a snake, he fought with his left hand down, his right hand devastating. His best years came in the 1980s, when his opponents—Pipino Cuevas, Wilfredo Benítez, Roberto Durán, and

THOMAS HEARNS—
Welterweight,
Junior Middleweight,
Middleweight and
Light-Heavyweight
Champion

Marvin Hagler—were more comparable adversaries. "I'm try-ing to sharpen up my speech," he said. "I have a tutor. She works with me on my English, spelling, how to use proper words. That way I can feel even more comfortable—I don't feel comfortable with strangers. I would like to get into acting. One goal is my secret to me. I do not desire to discuss it. I think it will happen, and I will be very successful. It will shock my fans. It's a matter of going out and pursuing it," he said. "But I want another title first. It will be hard for me to walk away if God tells me. I feel very strongly that God will give me a sign. I might just be walking around the streets, and He'll say, 'Thomas, it's enough.'"

"As a world champion, your life is not your own." said Marvin Hagler, the fierce southpaw who could adapt to any

TOMMY MORRISON—
Heavyweight
Champion

opponent's style. "You belong to the public. People think you're a doctor, a lawyer, a banker, that you can help them."

Like Roberto Durán, champions from other countries are heroes, kings, statesmen. They are touchable. Durán feeds an entire neighborhood and tries to aid everyone from a cottage behind his house in Panama. Julio César Chávez, aiming for one hundred fights so that he can retire, became a millionaire because of his jab and skillful boxing. A hero in Mexico, he signs autographs in the poorer neighborhoods and delivers gifts. "In Mexico, there are many important people," he said. "Politicians, actors, writers, and many others—but here I am the most important. It's incredible. I cannot believe it. Like Azumah Nelson is in Ghana, I am the king of boxing here." Once he was so poor that his family lived on boiled weeds. He used to wash cars and paint houses and now he owns three

JULIO CESÁR CHÁVEZ—Super Featherweight, Lightweight, and Super Lightweight Champion

HÉCTOR CAMACHO— Junior Lightweight and Lightweight Champion

buildings, two gas stations, "a lot of houses," and nineteen cars. "I go all around Mexico giving money and food to the poor people," he said. "I can't help all of them but I try. I came from poor people, that's why I do it."

Azumah Nelson, smoothing the sleeves of his mono-grammed silk pajamas in the late afternoon, called for another round of soft drinks from the throne on his porch. "I'm a big man here in small Ghana."

A dusty red-clay road with chickens pecking at its edges and craters the size of Volkswagens leads the way to the home of Nelson, a WBC super-featherweight and feather-weight champion. Pale green and orange lizards scale an eight-foot-high cement and metal fence that rings his proper-ty as one of Nelson's nine employees opens the gate solemnly and announces, "The champion is home." "Champion"'s home is a five-bedroom cement house with a living room as enor-mous as a department-store showroom; a kitchen filled with the most modern of gadgets and electrical appliances; a foun-tain with fish in the courtyard, separate quarters for his employees and for his cars, a swimming pool, and a barbecue. Glass, chrome, and sleekly styled wood furniture have been imported from prestigious department stores in Los Angeles and New York. A water-storage tank behind the house means that he has constantly running water, and when frequent power outages affect the neighborhood, he flees to a second of his five homes. Only a large wooden ceremonial mask attached to a wall and a cook beating plantains and cassava with a long wooden mallet into a local dish called fou-fou hint that this estate may be found in Ghana, a small country on the west coast of Africa. Cocoa, gold, and Azumah Nelson—pro-claimed the King of Boxing—are the country's greatest exports. When he defends his title away from home, a great crowd waves from the balcony of Accra's tiny airport as the hero departs and returns. Drums will pound and people will gather to eat, drink, and dance in front of his home in a show of sup-port, an idol with an image to defend and protect. Nelson once sold dresses, sugarcane, bananas—anything that could be placed on a tray and balanced on his head. Now he owns sev-eral businesses, including a brick-manufacturing company, a restaurant, and import-export companies, and he manages a

**AZUMAH NELSON—
Super Featherweight
and Featherweight
Champion, Ghana,
West Africa**

group of comedians. Ghanaians believe in his nobility, and they line up outside of his gate with requests for money (he gives), for advice (he offers), and to ask him to referee family squabbles (he does).

Nelson's profile is dignified, solemn, and graceful as befits a king; his voice is low and quiet. He seldom smiles. But he has a disarming and subtle sense of humor, a slow smile, and strong teeth. In the ring, he is like a compact spider, throwing punches from any angle, rarely hurt, and never discouraged. He fights three or four times a year since he turned pro in 1979, beating Wilfredo Gomez in 1984 for the WBC featherweight title. Nelson earned his reputation as a last-minute substitute in Salvador Sánchez's featherweight title bout in 1982; he gave Sánchez a hell of a fight, despite being stopped in the fifteenth and final round. He is promoted by Don King and has said that if it weren't for King, he would never have the wealth that he has. "Sometimes I feel like a slave," he admitted. "But what can I do?"

Another champion, Larry Holmes, complains loudly.

The bus station in Easton, Pennsylvania, is a plain storefront on the main street, with the floor of the waiting area covered by leaves blown in by the wind. It has many personalities. A sign lists apartments for rent and laminating services. There are bus tickets, arcade games, a change machine, and vending machines loaded with cheese and crackers mummified in plastic. Teenage girls draped over the pay phones drag on cigarettes in pale imitations of some 1950s chanteuse. You can buy a newspaper or wire money, and then sit on one of the hard wooden benches and watch a surly clerk who would rather be doing anything else.

Easton is the town that Larry Holmes belongs to; but since he owns so much property, it's more the other way around. The office of Larry Holmes, heavyweight champion, is located in Larry and Diane Holmes Plaza right off Larry Holmes Drive in this mostly-working-class city, two blocks from the bus station. To the south of his office, people trot off to make crayons at the Crayola factory. American Can is up the street along with factories and bakeries. "I used to walk across that bridge." Holmes points to a steel bridge that, if he turns around completely in his chair, he can see from the large pic-

**LARRY HOLMES—
World Heavyweight
Champion**

ture window. "I would shine shoes for two dollars. This building is my building. I own it." He doesn't talk fighting, he talks business. "People don't do what I did. They would have gone to the bank and taken out a mortgage. I don't owe one dime," he said proudly. "My house, my nightclub, my cars and boats. I have only one debt. I owe $120,000 on a $400,000 home in Jacksonville. That's the only debt that I have. That makes me independent. People don't want you to be independent," he insisted. "I can't do that. I worked so hard for this, I want the right to say yea or nay."

Holmes arrives at his office by noon, passing his awards nailed to the lobby walls and a large photograph of himself, and one of Dr. Martin Luther King, Jr., before he rides up in the elevator. Downstairs a bank and a federal court with three holding cells rent space from him. Photographs of his wife and children decorate the walls and desks. Seated at his desk, tasteful lavender carpet under his feet, his back faces a view of the river where the Lehigh empties into the Delaware. He has a conference room, a paper shredder, a large wooden desk and a fake cherry tree and a coffee cup with his name on it. He watches *The People's Court* before he goes to work and keeps up with the soap operas. He reads the newspapers and criticizes opponents of Dr. Jack Kevorkian, who assists in suicides. "With Dr. Kevorkian," he announced, "people have a right to kill themselves. If I want to drop off the building, let me go! I think people should mind their own damn business."

Holmes never left Easton. "I'm scared," he said with a little laugh. "I've lived here practically all my life. I know the ground, and I can go where I need to go." The telephone rings. It's his brother Mark, who boxed for a little while, and who is serving five years in prison for selling cocaine. Mark calls his brother collect, and then Larry connects them both with their mother, Flossie. "Hey, Mom!" he teases his mother. "So who's your favorite son? What do you mean it's not me!"

The telephone rings again and again until, finally, he is off the telephone. He begins flipping through a boating magazine. "It's one-upmanship," he said. "You've got to keep up with the Joneses. I had five Rolls-Royces, two limos, a bus—a total of seventeen cars and trucks. I said, 'What the hell am I doing?' I now have seven cars. We can't drive everything.

That's money that I put in the bank or put away for my kids.
You can only be in one room at a time."

Holmes, a mobile heavyweight with a fair chin who could
win a fight on his jab alone, turned pro in 1973 and didn't lose
a bout until 1985, when he lost his world heavyweight title to
Michael Spinks. He had defeated Ali, Trevor Berbick, Michael's
brother Leon, and Gerry Cooney before that. "Boxing is mind-
boggling. I was fighting fifteen rounds. And they criticize me,"
he complained. "I never stood there and took the punches.
That ain't Larry Holmes. Larry Holmes don't take no punches."
And then he met up with Earnie Shavers.

"Earnie Shavers"—Holmes shook his head—"that was
some tough sucker." In their second fight, Shavers knocked

him down with a right hand, and Holmes dropped as if he had been shot. But he managed to get up, stopping Shavers to keep his title. "When I fought Earnie Shavers, people thought that I had a lot of money. People wanted me to invest, to give them money—that's not about me. People think that it's fun to walk around Las Vegas and ask you for your autograph. They think I'm God. I ain't into that. It's nice to be important, but I want to be me. But when I don't want to be nice . . . well, I'm always nice. Someone always tries to take advantage of my kindness."

Holmes was a victim of the times. He came along right after Ali, but he never had that one opponent—that one fight—that would be his signature. Although he fought Ali and beat him, Ali was not in his prime; in fact, Ali had only one more bout before he retired in 1981. Ali had Liston, Frazier and Norton, and later Bowe had Holyfield; Holmes never had that one opponent who would make him a legend.

At forty-five, his face is a little fleshier than it used to be, his body and his haircut just a little rounder. His dark eyes look at the world belligerently. If the telephone rings, he can pick and choose his fights when others can't. "My drive is not that strong. Oh, I have it," he clarified. "But I don't have to sacrifice to work. Even though I'm forty-five years old, if I'm 100 percent, I'm better than a lot of people out there."

Holmes admits that because he is outspoken, he is not very well liked. "No one wants to get close to me. They're jealous. Promoters don't like me because I'm accomplished. I negotiate deals in my best interest. If I give someone 33 percent of my purse, he'll have to work. I give you what we agreed on—no more, no less. They give a manager 50 percent to call ten-second time, to wipe your sweat. Give a guy off the street $300. With the trainers—have they ever had a fight, ever taken a punch? I know how it feels to be punched, to be counted out, to be knocked down, to walk into that ring. I know how it feels to be hurt—your hands hurt, your back hurts, your feet hurt. They can't tell you what a left hook feels like. Like in Judge Wapner's court, they are there for moral support. Ferdie Pacheco—he's no expert. Muhammad Ali should tell him to shut the hell up. Angelo Dundee can't tell you what it feels like to get punched. Richie Giachetti can. I say it to them, 'You

The Contender, Fifth Street Gym, Miami Florida

don't know what it feels like.' They all cut each others' balls to get what's out there. I know what's best for me.

"I save my money. Put it to good use. I'm an independent fighter," he concluded. "Why do you think I'm fighting? The glory? The agony of defeat? You show a man who says he ain't fighting for money and I'll show you a fool."

Others, like Wimpy Halstead, Harold Brazier, and Don Johnson had to worry about bus fare. They never set out to be an opponent, just as an actor never decides to be an understudy. It just happened that way. To these journeyman fighters, the allure of boxing is read as simply dollar signs and nothing more. Some have second jobs. And with once-a-week shows in the Midwest, they can have over 100 fights, like Buck Smith. A few hundred dollars for several minutes' work will pay a bill or two, buy groceries or clothing for the kids. Johnson's career was one of bit parts and last-minute replacements, of promised leads and moonlighting under an assumed name. "Being that it gives me money, I do it to pay the bills," he said. "I never even think of becoming world champion."

As Johnson enters the footlights of the ring, the Armani suits and the Ferraris are about as far south of the Cross Bronx Expressway as you can get. His dark blue Camaro circa 1975 needs foot-stomping pushes on the gas pedal to start up; it's missing a radiator grille, and the rust holes on the hood add a little drama. You can drown in the holes in the seats and the windows crank wearily up and down. His sweatshirt, jeans, and clean white socks are straight off the rack while the sunglasses add a touch of mystery. He has no partner, carries no weapons. The only fighting he does is for a paycheck.

"They use him like a guinea pig," says his trainer, Angel Viruet. "He's an old-timer who hurt his chances when they were using him to bring other people up."

Johnson says that he's fought so many times that his opponents are difficult to remember. He turned pro in 1977. From 1979 through 1982, he fought under assumed names under the guidance of an unscrupulous manager. "I thought I was going to go somewhere," he said naively.

Johnson said that he was good enough as an amateur to be invited to the Amateur Athletic Union (now the Amateur Boxing Federation) championships in Florida in 1976. Fate was

GLENWOOD "The Real Beast" BROWN—Junior Welterweight Contender

against him in the person of Sugar Ray Leonard. "I fought three times a day there. That's when Sugar Ray Leonard was coming up. In the Olympics, you had to have a lot of money from a sponsor. So I had to come home. I hated him for that. We were both junior welterweights, but we never met. He had people to publicize and sponsor him. He looked at it as a business. I looked at it as a game. Maybe that's where I went wrong," he pondered. "He knew how to sell himself. I thought that the fight would sell me, but it doesn't."

He says he fought 150 amateur fights and, as a professional, went to Venezuela under the name of Ramírez. "I didn't speak Spanish, and no one bothered checking," he said. "I fought in a barn. I went to Puerto Rico three or four times. I had to dodge pots and pans." He worked in construction from 1983 to 1986. "I was looking for the easiest way out. I was making $18 an hour and looking for a raise to $21." He met and married Daisy Moy just as he resumed his career. On their first date, she rode behind him on his motorcycle, wearing her graduation gown and high heels, carrying her degree in cosmetology from The Wilfred Academy of Beauty. Johnson says that his record was 21–9, but it may really be 8–20. "Oh, now," he protests, "some of the records are wrong. Some of the losses are actually wins. And the 21–9 record includes the times that I fought as someone else."

Johnson got lucky once, knocking out an opponent on three days' notice. Six weeks later, he was knocked out in the second round with five days' notice and received a few hundred dollars. He arrived at a fight in construction clothes on one day's notice and lost a decision. His largest payday was a far cry from Sugar Ray Leonard's. He said that he earned $2,500 for a ten-round draw against the former International Boxing Federation junior middleweight champion Mark Medal, after which Medal retired.

Johnson's wife became his manager. He had no health insurance, life insurance, unemployment benefits, or job security. "I need to earn a living," he said. "Maybe we can afford to go on a cruise—in about thirty years."

Mike Tyson earned more in one fight than these opponents dare think about. Tyson, never the heir apparent to Muhammad Ali because of his brutish behavior in and outside the

MIKE TYSON —World Heavyweight Champion

**JUNIOR JONES—
Bantamweight
Champion**

ring, nevertheless captivated the public and television and earned $80 million. "Hey, it's just a job," he said. Joe Frazier laments that he and other world champions were unable to offer guidance and support to Tyson when he fell under the spell of Don King. "Mike Tyson could have been helped much more if he had the right kind of people at his doorstep, not in his corner. A lot of us were sitting around," Frazier said from his gym in Philadelphia. "I wish I had done something. But you're dealing with cobras and real black snakes, and you don't want to be a part of it. Floyd [Patterson], Muhammad [Ali], Emile [Griffith], Michael Spinks, George Foreman—we should have been there to support the man. Out of respect for the leader [Don King], we didn't. We didn't offer. We didn't *do* anything. It's sad that we didn't do nothing about it. You're just as wrong then. We didn't voice an opinion."

Eighty million dollars is difficult to comprehend. Roberto Durán started fighting just as Ali ushered in a wealthier age of television in boxing, and he watched the prize money climb higher and higher. The huddle around the television set to watch Friday-night fights has evolved into slick pay-per-view broadcasts bringing million-dollar purses. Where else can a man from the streets of Baton Rouge or Bedford-Stuyvesant or

Buenos Aires earn $10 million for (not counting training) less than one hour's work? For the purist and for the journalist, television has become the villain. It has turned club fighters into understudies, understudies into stars, and stars into superstars. Fighters moved to the suburbs and put up fences. The prizes vary wildly owing to amateur titles, weight class, maneuvering, and a little bit of luck. A club fight—no television, selling your own tickets as part of your prize—may net $200 for a pro debut. Oscar de la Joya, an Olympic gold medalist, earned over $50,000 for a televised pro debut. It took the junior welterweight and welterweight champion Buddy McGirt ten years to earn a million-dollar purse.

Instead of eight classes, there are now sixteen. World championships have been divided into three or more titles, and rarely consolidated into one. So, instead of one World Series or one Super Bowl, there are several. And for each middleweight who declares himself champion after his bout, there are four more sitting in the audience.

Television revenues pay the purses. Dangling huge sums of money, television created greed and, in turn, increased the number of sanctioning organizations from two to five or six, confused the public as to titleholders, invented idols, created overblown egos, and diminished the role of newspapers, magazines, and radio.

Fighters no longer need writers the way they once did. They used to wait for sportswriters to give them a nickname; now they create their own. When there were half a dozen newspapers in town and fights were as big as presidential elections, prizefighters would submit to interview after interview eagerly; all photographers had to do was name the time and place and pose. Now, Riddick Bowe can spend three minutes with a television crew and be exposed to millions of viewers with minimal effort. Deadlines and schedules are dictated by television; writers must wait until television dictates the start of the fight; delays can cause havoc with deadlines. Television represents money; newspapers and magazines do not. And, instead of boxers honing their craft by fighting several times a month, three or four times a year is average.

"I had more fights in one year than many of these guys have in their entire careers," said Jake LaMotta, who fought twenty bouts in 1941. "Leon Spinks—when he fought for the championship in his eighth fight, I was still fighting four rounds. Today, they don't have enough experience. They're not fully developed yet. It's very rare to see someone with thirty or forty fights."

"I don't think the heavyweights even have a slight resemblance to guys that I fought—Muhammad Ali, George Foreman, Sonny Liston, Ernie Terrell, Buster Mathis . . . ," Chuck Wepner complained. "Now they have five different rankings. It sounds like sour grapes, but there are too many champions. I very rarely watch fights anymore."

It *is* oversaturation. Fighters who, thirty years ago, could have been just a name in a record book, now contend for championships. And instead of fighting twenty-seven fights a year, as Henry Armstrong did in 1937, or Beau Jack, who fought three main events at Madison Square Garden in one month, two fights a year is not uncommon, ten fights rare for modern champions. They fight only when they have to. Liston and Foreman won titles, lost them, and never fought more than once or twice a year until they made comebacks. They were busier in their comebacks than in their prime. Even Tyson cut down to twice a year. An exception is Julio César Chávez who fights every six weeks or so, on average. Enormous purses have taken away boxers' hunger and overindulged them. Fighting used to be a job: to pay rent, to buy clothes, to put food on the table. Now it has turned fighters into new-money millionaires, like Riddick Bowe, who has to decide how many barbershop chairs to put in a new home.

"If I was forty-five, I might consider it with all that garbage out there," Wepner mused. "At fifty-five, they'd never license me. They're so flabby these days," he pointed out. "They have breasts like women. If I looked like that, I would be mortified."

And for the fan, it means having to spend more money. Higher-priced tickets—$50 seats, telescope not included, and $800 to $1,200 ringside seats in the bright lights of the casinos—fights shown on premium channels add on to the cable bill with pay-per-view shows at $20 to $40 plus. "With today's economy, thirty-six bucks? That's food for people!" Buddy McGirt scoffs. "Why waste it on ordering a fight? I think that there should be a limit," he said of fight purses. "I can't spend

**Fighter—
The Dominican
Republic**

78

$100 million. I don't think that any athlete deserves $30 million—to hit a baseball? Today's fighters? I don't find nothing. Not a damn thing. They all do the same thing. Jab, right hand, a left hook, and fall down. They don't deserve it."

Bobby Czyz, a cruiserweight and light-heavyweight champion who carries himself like a seasoned politician, commented, "I'm considering moving up just for the ha-ha. For $2 million, I'd fight an old lady with a kickstand—nothing personal." He was admitted to Mensa, an organization of people with the highest IQs. "I know I'm bright—I'm not the stereotype," he said. "I'm pretty much on Showtime the rest of my days. I'm 31—I'm not going to be George Foreman. I've been offered two jobs as a Wall Street broker. I'm looking for two or three more nice big paydays—a heavyweight ha-ha—and then I'm bowing out."

Bowing out when the final curtain falls usually means a few false starts and few more curtain calls. The prizefighter is usually the last one to catch on. First the legs go, then the reflexes, and finally the punch. He may have the heart, but his timing is off; he sees moves but can't get out of the way. He retires, and then retires again, hoping to be resurrected with some sort of eternal elixir.

Some men were born to paint, others to write, some to lead, and these men to fight.

"I don't care too much for boxing," admitted Michael Spinks, who won an Olympic gold medal, the world light-heavyweight title, and the world heavyweight title. "It's work. I would accept it if people would look at it a little differently. It's an art form, and it teaches you so much. You don't run into too many fighters who are egotistical. Boxers are very humble, very nice people, but they're viewed as brutes who are not too educated. I resent that. It's because of what they do for a living. We're just like everybody else, except we box for a living."

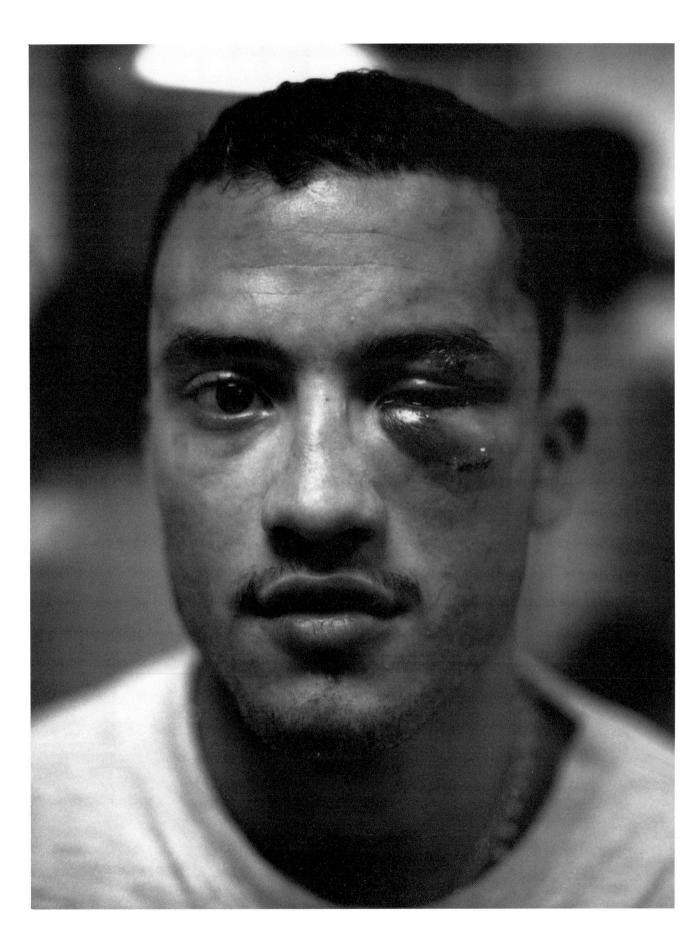

3

THE FIGHT

LIKE A GRAND Shakespearean play performed to the hilt, boxing has its heroes and villains, stars and bit players, knaves and rascals, and kings and their courtesans; from the heavy-weight clutching a crown to his worshipful attendant hoisting a bucket filled with spit. From the courageous and the cowards, the devious to the deviants, jesters and fools, tragedies, comedies and farces, myths and fairy tales, sonnets and swan songs, these are men of passion, lust, loyalty, and gullibility: schemers, poets, traitors who find good and evil in disguise. From the footlights to the spotlights, the beggars, peasants, kings, and princes of Shakespeare's plays have become the champions and contenders, the boxing ring their theater. And, as in many of Shakespeare's plays, in the end, the prizefighters, like heroes losing their nobility, become humble men.

Instead of coming from some distant castle, these men hail from the ruins of Bedford-Stuyvesant, the stockyards of Chicago, or the slums of Colómbia and Panama. Most are American blacks and Hispanics—Puerto Rican, Dominican, and Mexican; a few have come from Europe and Africa. The

PETE NIEVES—
Occupational Hazard

Friends

Jews and Italians have fled to the suburbs, more concerned with college, well-manicured lawns, and retirement plans than getting busted up in the ring. There are no Jack Dempseys, Benny Leonards, Rocky Marcianos, and Willie Peps anymore. Tommy Morrison is one of the few white men boxing professionally today. "There hasn't been any male bonding," he admitted. "I don't consider any of them friends. I'm a white fighter in a black-dominated sport. People have been told that white people can't fight. They are constantly questioning my ability to fight," he complained. "I don't think that I could ever do enough."

The fighters perfect their craft as baby-faced amateurs in small arenas and even smaller tournaments. The smallest amateurs clutch their trophies as firmly as the belt around the largest heavyweight, and they travel from tournament to tournament, many not even old enough to shave, and their voices crack when they tell you, shyly, that their dream is to become a champion. Their technique is awkward—all arms and legs—and, they rush out of corners like tiny tornadoes when the bell rings. Sometimes they are so scared that they close their eyes and flail away. So do their opponents. They have fathers who train them, coaches who assume the role of fathers, others

The Terminator

who scream and shout like Little League fathers, and some who don't know their sons at all. In high school, when other teenagers are playing basketball or studying chemistry or just hanging out, these young prizefighters pummel a speedbag, a heavy bag, or a sparring partner in the gym. They run before school in deserted streets and on cold tracks. They track each ounce more carefully than a socialite on a diet and wash and iron their fighting clothes and handwraps carefully. On the day of the fight, they are quiet, thinking of some far-off place where they, too, will have a title, a fancy house, a few cars, and a very large bank account. Some represent their country in tournaments overseas against foreign opponents; it is often their first airplane ride. A very select few make it to the

**JUAN LaPORTE—
Featherweight
Champion**

Olympics. The gold medal becomes their crown and instantly draws a steady line of managers and promoters. For others, like Mike Tyson, an Olympic gold medal probably wouldn't have made much difference. And when they turn pro, some are matched with men of equal skills and heart. A chosen few have carefully selected opponents whose destiny is to provide a little competition and nothing more.

The dressing room is where they find religion. Before a fight, it is a place of prayers, for questions, answers, and last-minute instructions. Tiger Flowers prayed, "Blessed be the

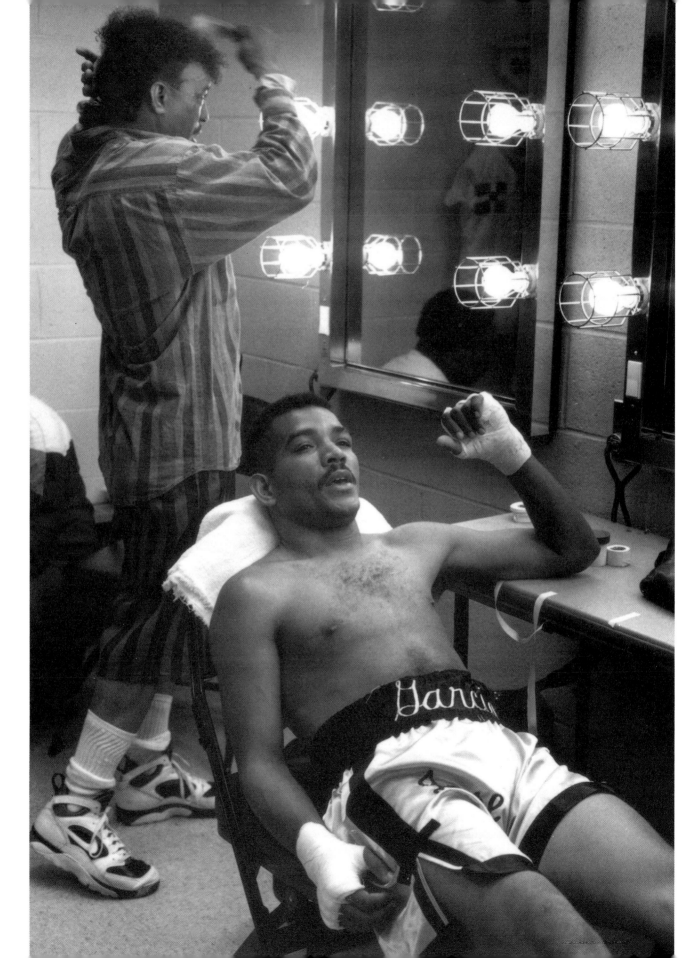

It's Over

Lord my strength, who teacheth my hands to war and my fingers to fight." Some stretch and sit quietly, their legs balanced on a chair in front of them, staring into space. Some, working off nervous energy, chat incessantly. These dressing rooms are barren, quiet places, unlike theatrical dressing rooms, with their pictures, props, and makeup. There are no mementos or frills here.

They would fight in the back of saloons, in cellars, in fields, any place that would set up a ring and collect bets before boxing was legalized in New York State in 1920 under the Walker Law. That became a model for similar laws in other states.

They fought in smoke-filled arenas like the Nostrand Athletic Club in Brooklyn, the Sunnyside Gardens in Queens, or Manhattan's St. Nicholas Arena; fifteen, twenty fights a year—sometimes as often as three times a month—for a few hundred dollars. Beau Jack, Henry Armstrong, and Sugar Ray Robinson were busy; it was almost an unwritten rule that you fought every five to six weeks. They perfected their skills—Johnson, Dempsey, Louis, Ezzard Charles, Saddler, Pep, LaMotta, Robinson, Marciano, Graziano—fighting in places like Yankee Stadium, Mexico City, Brooklyn, Caracas, Newark, Hartford, New Orleans, Cuba, Buenos Aires, and Salt Lake City. They had so much style then. Robinson was smooth and graceful in contrast to LaMotta's roughness. Their personalities echoed their fighting styles. Marciano would never stop coming at you, no matter how beaten or bloody. Saddler, who could hit like a heavyweight, had a rough style that forced Pep, a skillful boxer, to resort to that same roughness in order to survive. If you made any mistakes against Jack Dempsey, you paid for it. Gentleman Jim Corbett carried himself like—well, a gentleman, treating his opponents with respect. The soft-spoken Louis, the first black champion to be accepted worldwide, gave blacks a whole different way of being looked at, all because of his explosive hands. You could make one mistake against Joe Louis, but you couldn't make two. Dempsey, always a huge draw who brought in million-dollar gates, earned three times what Babe Ruth did. Later, Louis earned a few million more than Robinson, who still made quite a bit as a middleweight. And both had little when it came to the end.

The champions today fight in casinos and convention centers, swept into the ring by a mob of attendants, loud music, and gaudy outfits. Tyson ignored convention and entered the ring stripped to the basics, just as Dempsey did: a pair of black trunks minus a robe and socks. Others, like Héctor Camacho and Julio César Chávez, wear spangles, sombreros, tassels. Endorsements are hung on trunks and robes; they seem to be missing only from hair carvings and the soles of their shoes. Television cameras are everywhere and sometimes seem to intrude. Current and former boxers offer their analysis, and celebrities and newspapermen sometimes look as if they would rather be someplace else.

BERNARD HOPKINS—
Middleweight
Contender

And then the bell rings.

When the spotlight is turned on them, it is man down to the bare essentials.

"I psych myself," explained Riddick Bowe, a world heavyweight champion. "I'm the U.S., and I'm fighting for all the people to protect them. I consider my opponents to be from other countries, like Vietnam. Evander Holyfield—I consider him to be a big country, like Iraq. And the U.S. has to win."

"I don't want to knock my opponent out," Joe Frazier said. "I want to hit him, step away, and watch him hurt. I want his heart."

"Nothing can intimidate me," said Marvin Hagler. "I just go in and destruct and destroy."

"All I want to do is hit somebody in the mouth. It's a whole lot easier than working for a living," said Randall "Tex" Cobb.

"Don't make anything noble out of what I do."

"If anyone even dreams he can beat me, he had better wake up and apologize," said Muhammad Ali.

"Unless you've been in the ring when the noise is for you, there's no way you'll ever know what it's like," said Sugar Ray Robinson.

"When I'm in the ring, I forget the world exists," said Raymond González, an amateur fighter from New York City.

For Thomas Hearns and others, it is the challenge, the determination to outmatch the opponent, the joy of victory. "With my first title fight, people told me that it would be impossible to win," he said. "Then I went on to win more titles. I want to win another. I'm doing it for the money and because I love it—it's love and security even though I'm financially set for the rest of my life. To win—it's like no feeling that you ever had. To come in contact with a large sum of money which you never had—to finally get something. It makes you

very happy," he said, smiling to himself. "It's the greatest thing in the world. Everyone likes a winner. A winner is someone that people can congratulate, to honor. No one likes a loser. It hurts you deep inside. It makes you go home and think. I don't like suffering. It was hard for me to go into the street. I didn't want to be seen. You go home. You play everything back in your mind."

The lessons come from losing. "After eight years of victory as a professional, when I lost my title to Riddick Bowe, it did change something," Evander Holyfield admitted. "You wonder, 'What did I do so wrong? What caused this?' I felt like a rebellious kid. The last thing an athlete wants is to be embarrassed, to be wiped out. This is not supposed to happen to me. Deep inside, it was really eating me up. 'Did this guy really hit me this hard? Did I fight that lousy?' This is my art. I've worked to prove that I'm the best one out there."

"Lose?" asked Bob Foster, a world light-heavyweight champion who fought several times as a heavyweight. "Nobody likes to lose. When I lost to Joe Frazier, I wanted to win, and I cried and cried and cried. I tried to fight him, and when I did—well"—he threw up his hands—"all it takes is one mistake."

"I've had two different kinds of desires," explained Larry Holmes, heavyweight champion of the world from 1978 to 1985. "With Earnie Shavers, I was struggling, trying to accom-

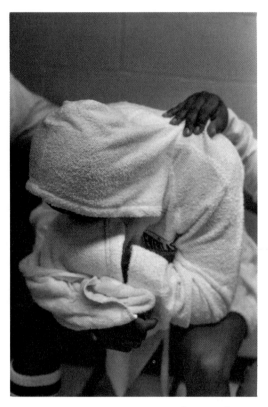

plish, trying to feed the hunger in myself. I worked very hard to do that. I sacrificed," he said. "Now I don't have to sacrifice. Even though I'm forty-five years old, they say that I'm taking away opponents for younger fighters. Why should I move aside when I'm able to do better? But when you lose a fight, you've got to come home and face your family and friends. Hey, I go home and have a party. Get drunk and talk about how I got my ass whupped. I'm going to the bank. There's always going to be someone a little bit better than you. You always want a second chance."

"When I lost the championship, I was very down," recalled Carlos Ortíz, a world junior welterweight and light-weight champion who fought from 1955 to 1972. "But everyone treated me the same. I was always a happy-go-lucky guy. I wasn't any different from being Carlos Ortíz."

Broken noses, cheekbones, jaws, and ribs, gashes, cuts, and bruises are what you might call the occupational hazards, whether a man earns $400 or $4 million. Sugar Ray Leonard, Larry Holmes, and Aaron Pryor suffered detached retinas. Michael Carbajal's scalp was sliced by a head butt. Punches thrown by Ken Norton broke the jaw of Muhammad Ali. A left hook by Joe Frazier broke George Chuvalo's eye socket. "When you get knocked out," observed Michael Spinks, who was knocked out by Mike Tyson, "it's like turning the lights off and then turning them back on. Your power is cut off. You have no more control. It's just black. It looks worse when you're trying to get on your feet. But it's not as painful as you would think."

"Knockouts?" repeated Archie Moore, who knocked out 141 men over four decades, the all-time record. "I felt pretty satisfied that I won the fight. I wasn't worried about the person. You can tell whether you hurt them or not. I was involved once in hurting a boy. I hurt him when I knocked him out. They took him to the hospital—he stayed for three or four weeks. I felt pretty badly when he was in the hospital, and I was hoping every day, every night, that he would come through. In the meantime, business went on. I kept my mind on my goals. It's a price you have to pay, chances you take in becoming a champion."

Managed by Charley Johnston and training at Stillman's Gym, Sandy Saddler was never short of work. "New York had a lot of fight clubs," Saddler recalled. "Sometimes I fought as often as three or four times a month. I'd go out and—boom, bang, bing. Jesus! I fought quite a bit." Some fighters these days would be happy with 10 knockouts. Saddler scored 103. "Boom, bang, bing! They were down!" he said. "But you get a feeling—you get scared. What if he couldn't get up?"

Some didn't.

Blood is the messiest problem—the hardest to handle—and it can take the fight out of the fighter. And that brings out the sorcerer—men like Ray Arcel, and Freddie Brown and later Ace Marotta, Eddie Aliano, Ralph Citro, and Al Gavin, who mixed potions to control bleeding and swelling.

Ray Arcel, who began his training career in the 1920s when cuts were plugged with chewing tobacco, used to climb through the ropes and into the ring, his mouth filled with swabs and a bag packed with scissors, tape, a sponge, and a stopwatch, Monsell's solution (a liquid placed on cuts to stop the flow of blood), beef broth, and brandy for the slow starters. "There is a secret to handling a fighter who is cut and bruised," said Arcel. "Some fellas get a small cut and they think they're gonna bleed to death. You have to know your fighter. Is the fighter able to handle the cut? Sometimes he'd go to pieces on you. The most sensitive human beings in the world are boxers."

Arcel accumulated twenty world champions and worked with over 2,500 fighters in his sixty-five years as a trainer. And one of his champions—Roberto Durán—is still boxing. ("I knew right away he was going to be a world champion," he said.) After eight or nine fights as a professional boxer for two-dollar purses, Arcel became a trainer at seventeen. He sent many men into the ring against Joe Louis, so many that Louis once stood across from him as the referee was giving instructions and queried, "You again?" Arcel trained the middleweight champion Tony Zale, welterweight champion Ted (Kid) Lewis, Barney Ross, who won the lightweight, junior-welterweight, and welterweight titles, and two heavyweight champions, Ezzard Charles and Larry Holmes, who was Arcel's last pupil before he retired in 1982 at the age of eighty-

**RAY ARCEL—
trainer**

three. "Each fighter was important to me," Arcel, who died in March of 1994, said. "I became a part of that fighter. No two fighters can do things the same way. Know their shortcomings and their idiosyncrasies and their physical makeup. And," he added, "always make sure you know about his opponent."

The most interesting fights are those which display contrasts in style. The boxer and the brawler, the attacker and the counterpuncher, uppercut against jab, the smooth stylist against the rough one, the fighter who would throw anything against a more cautious and respectful opponent, dirty fighters like Fritzie Zivic and Harry Greb, the master of every foul from a thumb in the eye to a knee in the groin, heart against intellect, tap dancers like Willie Pep against waltzers like Chalky Wright, old men like Archie Moore and Sonny Liston against young ones like Cassius Clay, slow starters against quick tempers, clean-cut images against dangerous ones, Dempsey and Tunney—the Marine versus the Manassa Mauler, Ali and Frazier—The Showman against the Working Man and Leonard against Durán—Good against Evil and Joe Louis versus Billy Conn—"He can run but he can't hide," Louis said of that 1941 bout.

Michael Spinks wanted to hide, but he couldn't. In ninety-one seconds, he was knocked out by Mike Tyson; he had been

the greatest hope at that time to beat Tyson—and the sense of anticipation was unmatched. Spinks never had a chance to set his feet properly. Then it was all over. "I used to be untouchable," he mused. "For Tyson—I was a wreck. Nothing was panning out. As the fight started to get closer, I kept asking myself, 'Is it going to work? Is it my time?' Fear was knocking on my door big time. I was afraid of what was going to happen to me. I didn't want to lose my life in the ring."

Boxing is style and anticipation and unpredictability. It can be a matter of catching an opponent off balance, of waiting for him to make a mistake, the willingness to fight, and the heart to mix and trade punches. Until he fought Sonny Liston, Ali's nineteen fights were nothing to rave about. Liston, a 7–1 favorite, was battered by Ali's combinations and did not come out for the seventh round. No one expected Leon Spinks to beat Ali in only his eighth fight. Tyson went straight to the kill, and would hug and kiss his opponents after he knocked them out. Then he was upset by Buster Douglas in Tokyo.

Moorer, Holyfield, Bowe, Holyfield, Douglas, Tyson, Spinks, Holmes, Ali, Spinks, Ali, Foreman, Frazier, Ali, Liston, Johansson, Patterson, Marciano, Walcott, Charles, Louis, Braddock, Baer, Carnera, Sharkey, Schmeling, Tunney, Dempsey, Willard, Johnson, Sullivan—the lineage is formidable. "The heavyweight is the most visible," Riddick Bowe

commented. "I think people respect the heavyweight champion of the world in that he's bigger and can respect everybody. The greatest thrill of all is to be recognized as the greatest heavyweight champion in the world. It's unique in itself. You see movie stars, princes, everyone gets into it with the heavyweight champion. It's a lot of work," he added.

Gene Tunney, who had enlisted in the Marine Corps during World War I and read Shakespeare, was a defensive fighter who wore down his opponents. He was not an attacker like Jack Dempsey. Dempsey left home as a teenager in Colorado and rode the rails in search of fights and wore a wild scowl in contrast to the impassive face of the clean-cut Marine. People would come to see Jack Dempsey lose; they hated him because he didn't go off to war and didn't defend his title for over two years. He became more popular after his career than during it.

Jack Dempsey lost his title against Tunney in ten rounds during pouring rain in Philadelphia in 1926. Tunney, clever and sharp, controlled the bout in every round except two, eliminating much of Dempsey's attack. They met for a rematch a year later, in the famous bout called "The Battle of the Long Count," and Dempsey lost by decision a second time.

Ali stole the show. He shouted his blackness to white America, stood up to the establishment by refusing to fight in the Vietnam War, and became a Muslim, a missionary, and a myth. Frazier was like the brooding, hardworking neighbor, mumbling a few words of greeting and trotting off to work every day with a metal lunch box and thermos, returning home to his wife and kids in the evening.

Muhammad Ali's three fights with Joe Frazier—in 1971 (Frazier by decision), 1974 (Ali by decision) and 1975 (Ali after fourteen rounds, when Frazier's trainer, Eddie Futch, threw in the towel)—still stand as the most dramatic and storied series in boxing history. They were brutal clashes inside the ring; Frazier bore in relentlessly as Ali sidestepped and countered, keeping his hands low and bouncing off the ropes. But in a war of words, it was Ali who bore in; Frazier, instead of countering, stood squarely in place.

"I am the greatest!" Ali shouted to the microphones.

"Gorilla!" He turned and spat at Frazier.

Frazier never laughed at Ali's words as Ali aimed for territory Frazier was not accustomed to defending. Ali picked on his opponent's muddy South Carolina drawl, his grammar, vocabulary, intelligence, and his blackness. Like most fighters,

Frazier was prepared for physical battle when the bell rang, not a verbal war of poems, prose, and insults, ringed by cameras, notepads, and microphones.

Whether prizefighters like it or not, Ali became boxing's greatest showman and role model. "I've seen a lot of fighters who want to be Muhammad Ali," said the trainer Eddie Futch. "There was once this tall, adequately built man. He would come into the gym with his long hair tied in the back. He was on his toes. He's shadowboxing, hitting the bag, skipping the rope, doing Muhammad Ali. Then he walked out of the gym. He wouldn't put on a pair of boxing gloves to save his life. He had copied Ali's style so well, but he never boxed anybody!" Futch continued, "Ali knew exactly what he was doing, and his attitude had a purpose. He wanted to get his opponent's mind on something else."

"I never downgraded my opponent," said Carlos Ortíz. "I never chastised them, I never threatened them like they do today. I would simply say that the fight is not going to go the distance. I would say it that way. They all copy Muhammad Ali. It was never like that before him. They started to imitate him and do all these shenanigans. It worked with Muhammad Ali—it won't work with anyone else. If you want to be a comedian, go into show business."

Mike Tyson never imitated Ali, but he studied and examined Ali and every other great fighter. He watched films, read books, asked questions, and listened. "I got lucky and discovered boxing and some good people who believed in me," he said, until he listened to the wrong voices.

In the dressing room after his fight with Holmes at the Atlantic City Convention Center, a sweat-splattered mirror and a hole punched in the wall testified to Tyson's ferocity. The room was deserted. The training table was arranged neatly with ice buckets, water bottles, crumpled-up old towels, and neatly packaged fresh ones. A few soda cans were tossed into one corner. Across the stage on which the Miss America pageant takes place, the mirror in which Larry Holmes looked himself in the eye stood spotless and empty. His dressing room looked as though a party had taken place, in contrast to the workmanlike stillness of Tyson's. Holmes's training table, pushed to an odd angle, was covered with footprints and dirty

towels. Cans of soda, bottles of water, and more dirty towels covered the floor. A broken bottle lay next to the mirror. Under two towels in the corner were two copies of a tape that Holmes presumably had listened to before his fight against Tyson: Holmes singing his rap song, "You Can't Keep a Good Man Down." But Tyson did. For just under twelve minutes' worth of work, Holmes collected $3 million.

"Why am I coming back?," Holmes asked. "I'll make a long story short: M-O-N-E-Y."

"Small guys can't raise any hell," Muhammad Ali once said. But they have.

Roberto Durán is much smaller than expected in person, but his dark eyes and square face reveal nothing. His hair grows black and wild, and there are no gray hairs in his neatly trimmed mustache. He wears a size-nine boxing shoe, and his body has seen the schizophrenia of his appetite. He does not have the legs of a young man, but they are not an old man's legs, either. He is slower than some, still faster than many. A fighter of passion, soul, and machismo, he fought his way out of the streets of Panama, a third-grade dropout who once

ROBERTO DURÁN

knocked out a horse. He knocked down men and was greeted by parades and by presidents. He was nicknamed "Manos de Piedra" or Hands of Stone and ignited all of Panama into a jubilant frenzy when he brought home the lightweight title in 1972. He drove in motorcades with bodyguards, bought a house and invested in real estate, and seemed a little surprised by it all. The parades are gone and so, they say, is much of the money. So, he still fights at forty-three, his hard eyes still finding openings for his punches and the weaknesses of his opponents. Roberto Durán's hands are surprisingly soft; square and a little plump, with a fine coating of black hairs and tiny half-moons rising on carefully trimmed fingernails. "Aah, like baby's skin," he croons, rubbing the back of his hand against a young woman's. His knuckles are lumpy, broken, calcified. His palms are smooth and warm and display lines that a fortune-teller might say indicate a long, productive life.

And Roberto Durán has lived a long, productive life. He now fights in places like Bay St. Louis, Mississippi, and Buffalo, New York, and trains in towns like Erie, Pennsylvania. In Erie, a freight train rumbles overhead as he runs under a musty bridge, pigeons scattered by his footsteps, his breath misty in the dank air. Durán emerges from the tunnel, perhaps recalling his early days fighting for $25 in Panama City. He runs through a town painted a somber gray punctuated by bright lights of fast-food chains, where the finest homes are funeral parlors and where tired work shirts hang for sale in thrift shops.

To earn his first title, Durán mauled Ken Buchanan, who lost his title on a technical knockout in the thirteenth round. Glaring, Durán would insult his opponents and their families and, when he knocked them down, he spat on them. His first loss was a nontitle fight with Esteban de Jesús but he redeemed himself by knocking out de Jesús a year and a half later. They met a third time in 1978, when he knocked de Jesús out again to retain his title in Panama. The last time he put his arms around de Jésus was in 1989, when de Jesús was dying of AIDS in a hospice in Puerto Rico. Durán embraced his old foe and wept.

Durán fought Sugar Ray Leonard, the 1976 Olympic gold medalist who wore a photograph of his girlfriend—later his

wife—taped to his socks during the Olympics. Smooth and likable, if not a little remote, Leonard was a product of extensive amateur training and competition. Some people called his flamboyant style reminiscent of Ali. In 1980, in Montreal, Durán, a serious, focused fighter with murderous eyes, took Leonard's world welterweight title away from him in a fifteen-round decision. The president of Panama sent a plane for Durán. Wearing a white suit and a bewildered expression, he was greeted by mobs and paraders anxious to touch him. He drove through Panama City with escorts to the president's palace, six policemen on each side. Television sets replayed the fight over and over again. Five months later, Durán fell from grace. Perhaps frustrated by Leonard's taunting but insisting that he had cramps, Durán threw up his hands and said, *"No más"*—no more. Panamanians had bet their furniture and homes on him, and pride and the fear that he betrayed his countrymen kept Durán from returning to Panama immediately after that fight.

Durán hung the WBA portion of the junior middleweight championship belt in his home in Panama in 1983, after stopping Davey Moore. He fought Marvelous Marvin Hagler for Hagler's undisputed middleweight title and lost, but later added the WBC middleweight championship belt to his collection, outpointing Iran Barkely for the title in 1989. Durán was thirty-eight and the underdog.

Durán fought Leonard a third time, this time in 1989, losing a lethargic twelve-round decision for Leonard's WBC super middleweight title. Indifferent and spiritless, Durán blamed the loss on his weight and Leonard's insistence that the fight be held at 162 pounds, not at 168. "I lost too much weight too quickly," Durán explained. "I was overconditioned. I expected the fight to be at 168, and then found out that it was 162. That was Leonard's wish; he's like a spoiled child. And because of Leonard's 'Mr. USA'—we have to play by his rules. Ray's the boss." Durán earned close to $7 million for that bout.

In 1992, Durán weighed 220 before slowly working off the extra weight and was billed as a living legend. He insists, "It is not for the money, but because I want to fight. I'm chasing my fifth title, and that will be my last fight. I'm coming back to prove to people that I can fight. Age is a big factor, but my expertise balances it out. Money is not the issue. My financial problems are in the past. Everybody works for money. Fighting is a business, and you get paid for it."

Durán won his 100th bout, this time as a super middleweight, in December 1993 against an opponent half his age whose father was Durán's own age. "Sometimes the father talks more than the son," he laughed. "He's not the one that gets his ass kicked. They all say, 'Do this, do that.' Let the father get in the ring." Durán's first professional fight was in 1967 when he was fifteen, five years before his opponent, Tony Menefee, was born. "The one hundreth is very important," he said before a small crowd that included his promoters and friends. "Not many people made it to one hundred fights. Thank God that I have all my reflexes." He looked at the ceiling and back again. "I want to be known as the greatest fighter of all time. I've been rated number two behind Sugar Ray Robinson. I think I deserve to be number one."

Durán stayed at the Days Inn in Diamondhead, Mississippi, to prepare for this 100th fight. As he jogged around a golf course in the morning and headed back to the hotel, he would pass a Dairy Queen on his left and he ran right through the lobby of the building, his trainer and an assistant holding open the doors so that he wouldn't have to break stride. "Hi, hi," he called to the women at the front desk. The fight would take place in two days, in Bay St. Louis, Mississippi, at a place called Casino Magic.

Later that evening, lying naked under the blankets pulled up to his waist, Durán said that he planned to run for the senate in Panama. "And boxing, too. I have a secretary." A legend who often flies coach, Durán complained about his last plane ride. A man sitting next to him asked him to turn out the light. So Durán did, but showed off a little book light that he purchased later to attach to his head like a miner's lamp. "See!" he said proudly. "Now I won't disturb anyone." He admired a writer's watch and then lamented that he had bought the same watch—different style—but liked hers better. He stopped everything, pulled a black nylon bag onto his lap, and began searching for his watch. "I got a camera, I got two cameras," he said, removing items from the bag. "Hey, look at this cigarette lighter!" He flicked open an erotic cigarette lighter more appropriate for a bachelor party. "I bought it for a friend back home who likes these kinds of things. I paid a dollar for it," he said, laughing to himself. His crowd reacted as he did. "Sunglasses!" He tried them on, to everyone's approval. "Look, I got tapes, I got a Walkman, here are some vitamins, and here are more vitamins." He searched through the bag, but found no watch. "Better watch it—I'm fast," he warned, glancing at the writer's watch. Finally the crowd was ushered out by one of his promoters, and Durán waved good-bye.

"He is very unpredictable," commented one member of his group. "That is why promoters have so much trouble dealing with him. You never know how he is going to be."

While Durán's eyes don't look menacing anymore, he is still unpredictable. He entered the ring in a shiny black satin robe with a gold rope belt and four crowns embroidered, his name down the side of his shorts and his shoes in gold. He beat Tony Menefee the following evening, knocking him down in the fifth

round and dominating the fight until the bout was stopped in the eighth. "After one hundred fights, I have learned patience," Durán said afterward. "The hardest person to fight is the one who just wants to survive by running away."

Menefee was brave. He slipped through Durán's defense to land a harmless punch or two and backed up, but didn't run away. Durán caught him in the eighth, first with combinations to his body and then with a hard right to the head. Menefee seemed suspended for a moment; then he collapsed onto the canvas like overcooked spaghetti. He struggled to rise, supported by the ropes. When he finally did, the referee motioned for the bout to continue. Durán motioned to the referee to stop the fight. "I didn't want to kill him," he said, sounding not quite menacing. He opened his arms to the crowd, and then moved to embrace Menefee, who, unhappy that the fight was stopped, did not touch him. Four men hoisted Durán off the floor, and he waved. "If the referee hadn't stopped it, that kid would have been in the hospital," he said. "I signaled to the referee because he's a young fighter, an up-and-coming guy, and I didn't want to hurt him. If they hadn't stopped it, I could have killed him. He was out on his feet."

"He is the real king of macho," said Mike Acri, his promoter. "He beat Barkley and he beat Hagler when Hagler was an animal. He's not afraid of anybody. This is what he wants to do," he insisted. "This is what he does for a living. It's not a sad story. Sure, I made a good piece of change with Durán. But I didn't ask him to fight. He contacted me. So—he spends a little money. He's always short on cash, but he's put away money until the year 2000."

"He misused it," Ray Arcel said. "He had bad advice, bad investments. But I root for him. Some of us are blessed with tremendous talent. You don't lose it. And I think he may know more about boxing than I do."

Trainer Esteban Frías offers Durán pointed reminders, not instructions. Durán's wife, Felicidad, a soft-spoken blonde of thirty-eight, watched her husband spar. "I have a lot of confidence in him," she said. "But I always get a little nervous when he's fighting. I always pray that nothing happens to him. Once he gets in training and starts to drop the weight, he always gets a little irritable. I give him more support at that time."

Felicidad was fourteen and in love with a young fighter of nineteen with a string of knockouts when they met twenty-four years ago. She, too, has had a life of training camps, hotel rooms, and ringside palpitations. She always traveled to her husband's bouts with their children. Now the children are older and attend school in Panama. The oldest, twenty-one-year-old Roberto, Jr., plays basketball and studies law; his sisters, Jovana, nineteen, and seventeen-year-old Irichelle love soccer. Thirteen-year-old Roberto III would like to be an actor. Víctor Roberto, who is almost three, hits anything with a miniature jab, blocks his face with one fist, and calls women *puta* ("whore" in Spanish).

"There are times when I have asked my husband to retire, and he says no," Mrs Durán admitted. "He himself only knows when to stop. When his mind is set on something, he is determined."

Durán feels that the date of his baptismal certificate may be wrong, due to an error made by his grandfather, and he is still waiting for a copy to arrive from Panama. "Hopefully," he said, "I'll be a few years younger." He laughs heartily. "Maybe I'm really twenty-five."

But he is not twenty-five. He is forty-three.

The tragedy for all boxers is that they, too, grow old. *Et tu?*

4

THE FINAL ROUND

A PRIZEFIGHTER'S life is a short one. Sometimes, with several lifetimes wrapped into one, he leaves the spotlight—bewildered, forgotten, broke. There is no crowd, no applause, no one waiting for an autograph; the toughest men in the ring leave the most vulnerable. The daily routine and incentives are gone, and so is the manager who planned the details. And, as in Shakespeare's plays, it is a tragedy; the prizefighter, a man of superior skills, humbled, overcome by one large and stubborn obstacle: himself.

"You always say, 'I'll quit when I start to slide,' and then one morning you wake up and you've done slid," said Sugar Ray Robinson, who retired when he was forty-four.

"Thirty-six is getting to the age," remarked Muhammad Ali. "You know it's time to leave but something tells you you've got one more gamble."

Just as fighters have different beginnings, they have different endings. The image of the retired boxer can be a sad one: of fortunes squandered, mumbling to himself and touring the gyms, looking for a handout. But, like any stereotype, there is some truth to it, and it is not difficult to find a man to fit that image. To realize that this man, once the champion of the world, has been reduced to a mere mortal, is often more difficult for even himself to comprehend. His body, once a magnificent sculpture, turns to fat or shrivels and often bears no resemblance to what it used to be. Joe Louis was a tourist attraction at Caesar's Palace; at the end, seated in a wheel-

chair, ill and unaware of his surroundings, he became a cardboard cutout for tourists to pose with.

Some fighters are content to live off their fame. Some turn to God. Others find themselves unsuited for anything but boxing so they become managers and trainers. But many have settled into a myriad of occupations. Joe Louis was just going to play golf and live off his money until he ran short and had to pay the IRS. Tony Zale worked in youth centers around Chicago. Benny Brisco became a sanitation worker. Eddie Mustafa Muhammad trains fighters. Billy Fox worked in construction. Henry Armstrong became a minister; Benny Leonard a boxing referee; Mickey Walker an artist. Willie Pep does publicity work for a casino in Connecticut. Carmen Basilio worked for his brother's sausage company, became athletic director of LeMoyne College, and now makes appearances for Genesee Brewery in upstate New York. Donald Curry manages and trains fighters. Archie Moore devoted his life to helping underprivileged youth, driving a truck and picking up donations of meat and produce and delivering it to families. Named by President Reagan as special ambassador to the Watts section of Los Angeles, Moore worked with youth groups until kids started toting Uzis. He still speaks

JERSEY JOE WALCOTT—World Heavyweight Champion

to students and filmed a commercial for the United Way. Jersey Joe Walcott became a boxing commissioner. So did Floyd Patterson, who trains his son, Tracy. Jack Dempsey owned a restaurant. Maxie Rosenbloom, who had 299 fights, became an actor and owner of a nightclub called Slapsie Maxie's. George Chuvalo sold real estate and has his own TV show in Canada. Sean O'Grady and Barry McGuigan became television commentators. Howard Davis, Jr. became a construction worker, vitamin salesman, and boxing trainer; Leo Randolph, a truck driver, and Max Schmeling the owner of a Coca-Cola distributorship in Germany. Hilmer Kenty owns his

SUGAR RAY ROBINSON—World Welterweight and Middleweight Champion

own electronics parts company in Detroit, Kenty Electronics. Michael Olajide, Jr. teaches his own blend of boxing and aerobics. Joey Giardello works with the mentally handicapped. Vito Antuofermo owned Champ's Pizza, made a few movies, and attempted to make a comeback. Primo Carnera became a successful wrestler; Eder Jofre, a politician in São Paulo; and Billy Backus, a deputy commissioner of the New York State Athletic Commission, is a supervisor for Marcy Prison in upstate New York.

In the old days, from the late 1800s to the early 1900s, some, like John L. Sullivan and Jim Corbett, toured the vaudeville circuit. The next generation showed up in bit parts in movies, from Barney Ross and Maxie Rosenbloom to Víctor McLaglen, who fought an exhibition against Jack Johnson and later won an Academy Award as Best Actor for *The Informer*. Lou Nova became a stage and screen actor, Sugar Ray Robinson sang and danced a bit on television, but his name was greater than his talent in between retirements. Randall "Tex" Cobb makes movies and commercials. Mark Breland studies acting and has performed in television and in films. Ray Mancini, a bit actor in the movies,

VITO ANTUOFERMO— World Middleweight Champion

onstage, and on television, has set up his own production company. George Foreman starred as himself in a weekly sitcom. Marvelous Marvin Hagler now speaks with an Italian accent and lives in Italy, where he has appeared in several movies. "I miss being punched. Seriously," he insisted, still bald and still in shape. "I really love the art of boxing, hitting the other guy. And it's the pain, too," he added. "It's the pain that really helps you. But I said, '*ciao.*' I don't want to work in a hotel, like Joe Louis."

Carlos Monzón sits in prison, serving time for killing his girlfriend. Mike Tyson, Trevor Berbick, and Tony Ayala were convicted of rape, John Tate of possession of drugs. "Bad dream?" asked Ayala, a former junior middleweight contender.

RAY MANCINI— Lightweight Champion and Father, Leonard

"It's been too hard to be a bad dream. I don't think about what could have been. Tragedy would have occurred anyway."

They think it's going to last forever. It's easy to spend the money but the lifestyle is difficult to maintain when the money isn't coming in anymore.

Some fighters retire firmly, other reluctantly, and some more than once. A retirement without a few comebacks is rare. They find themselves fighting opponents young enough to be their sons and losing to opponents they would have dispatched in one round years earlier, waking up the next morning, the fatigue and ache of old wounds a reminder that this is not a game for old men. When the fighting is over finally and completely, gone are the competition, the regimentation,

**TONY AYALA—
Rahway Prison,
Former Junior
Middleweight
Contender**

**MARVIN HAGLER—
World Middleweight
Champion**

the adulation, and the money. Boxing doesn't offer Social Security or job security. Teachers, writers, cabdrivers, computer programmers, bankers, and shoe salesman can keep teaching, writing, driving, programming, banking, and selling past the age of sixty-five. But, on average, by the time fighters reach their early thirties, the boxing lifetime is over.

For most of the last two generations of prizefighting champions and some of their opponents—Riddick Bowe, Evander Holyfield, Thomas Hearns, Michael Carbajal, Mark Breland, Sugar Ray Leonard, Julio César Chávez, Pernell Whitaker, Gerry Cooney—the money has been so great from the beginning that they never had a job, never had to punch a time clock, never had to answer to a demanding boss, never had a budget. "You're lucky," Emanuel Steward, who climbed telephone poles in the middle of winter for Detroit Edison, told Thomas Hearns. "You've never had to work for a living."

The fate of all these prizefighters is still unknown.

Leonard made a workout video, and does a little television commentary and casino public relations. Breland teaches a few fitness classes and trains a few dogs. Michael Spinks helps out his former promoter, Butch Lewis. Buster Douglas retired; he goes fishing and watches movies. "I never retired," Breland insisted. "The papers retired me." Usually reserved, he added that he was worried that when he retired, people would remember him as "a shitty person. Look at Sonny Liston. He was a shitty person. After you retire, who gives a shit? When you get old, someone else is going to take your place."

Gerry Cooney, the big, friendly Irish kid from the suburbs, carefully cultivated and manicured, brought a burden of hope, hype, and hoopla to the heavyweight scene but he couldn't carry it. He lost to Larry Holmes in 1982—his trainer throwing in the towel—when a booming left hook defeated him, his concentration muddled. With a wink and a smile, Cooney, a charmer who knows all the lines, seems bewildered and uncertain of himself. "I think I stayed in it too long," he admitted. "It seems like I have luck, but it's all bad." Cooney has managed and promoted a few fighters, and he owns a house with a swimming pool out in the Hamptons.

"He knew he blew his chances," said his trainer, Víctor Valle. "He could have been the greatest. Who the hell knows? A white fighter—God!"—he exclaimed—"he could have controlled New York City!"

"Money has made bums out of people," declared the trainer George Benton, a fighter from the streets of Philadelphia, so tough and fearless that he couldn't get opponents.

MARK BRELAND—
Welterweight
Champion

The story of Leon Spinks is one of the most dramatic; he came from nothing, zoomed to the top—decked in furs, tossing dollar bills, honking the horn of an expensive automobile—and plummeted back down, even farther and faster from where he began.

The Spinks brothers grew up poor in east St. Louis, Missouri. Their parents separated when Michael and Leon were young and they were raised by their mother. Michael said later, "If my father had been around, I think my life could have turned out differently. Maybe I wouldn't have become a professional boxer."

All Michael Spinks wanted to do was to follow his older brother, Leon, to the gym. But Leon, three years older, always beat him. Both are 1976 Olympic gold-medal winners and world champions. And there the similarity ends.

Leon joined the Marines before he turned pro in 1977. His ring style matched his personality—erratic; he looked great in some fights, awful in others. But if you pushed him around, he was easy to beat. In just his eighth fight, he stunned Muhammad Ali and everyone else by capturing Ali's world heavyweight title. Leon, the man with the toothless smile, was just twenty-four. Trained by George Benton and managed by Butch Lewis, the world was in their hands. Seven months later, Leon lost his title back to Ali.

Michael, a good boxer but one who didn't look it because of his awkwardness, beat Dwight Braxton in 1983 for the world light-heavyweight title, and then Larry Holmes in 1985 for the world heavyweight title. He was knocked out by Mike Tyson in 1988. As erratic as Leon's style and personality were, Michael's moves were more cautious, his personality warm, friendly, and polite with a knee-slapping sense of humor. He lives in Maryland with his daughter Michelle and keeps an apartment in Philadelphia, where he lived after he first signed a managerial contract with Butch Lewis.

Leon Spinks filed for bankruptcy in 1986, stating that all he had left from the $4.5 million he had won was a $500 wardrobe and the $1,600 a month he was currently earning from boxing. His championship belt auctioned, his "friends," late nights, fast women, and faster cars had consumed him. "They all moved too fast for me to pay attention to," he said. Although Leon insists that he still has his belt, a former lawyer said it

LEON SPINKS—
World Heavyweight
Champion

was auctioned off in December 1985 to pay his bills. Leon keeps talking about fighting again, but his license application keeps getting rejected; boxing commissions are not willing to license a former champion with diminished skills. He said that he does not ask for pity; it's his life.

After the Olympics, Butch Lewis signed Leon to a professional contract while Michael thought he would come home to a hero's welcome. "Mike was kind of disillusioned," Lewis said. "He just wanted a good job. They gave him a job at a major company—cleaning toilets. Were he a white gold medalist, they would not give him a job cleaning toilets. That pushed him over the edge. Leon wanted Mike to be with him. Mike wanted to come back to a hero's type of thing and go on with his life and retire with a twenty-five-year watch."

Lewis guided Michael to the light-heavyweight and heavyweight championships, instructed him on how to handle his finances—which he has maintained carefully—and has him work with his fight promotions. But his brother Leon's fame and fortune evaporated.

MICHAEL SPINKS and Daughter, Michelle

Michael observed, "Leon—if he didn't have a dime my love would never change. I'll sleep in the streets with Leon. We were like twins in the Olympics. We used to dress alike. We were just brothers.

"I miss the days of starting out poor—me and Leon. I miss the days of being together. I've missed him. Leon . . . it's unfortunate that these things happen. I saw us together for life, inseparable." He inhaled deeply and let it out sadly, closing his eyes heavily.

"One day we were taking a walk across a recreation center. No one was there—it was empty. I said, 'Leon, let's box.' We boxed for two-minute rounds—three rounds. I would cover up and he would box and then he would tire up and then I got my licks and hit him with punches and I hit him good. I got him! I ran out of the ring, hollering, 'I kicked your ass!' This was in 1972 or 1973. I was the happiest man alive."

Leon Spinks's fiery style and desire caught the attention of Butch Lewis, whose promotional juices started flowing at the idea of a brother team. He signed Leon to a professional contract, contacting him in the Marines and arranging for his discharge. Lewis thought he could manage Leon, but gave up just after Leon's rematch with Muhammad Ali. All at once, Lewis's voice sounds strained, angry, and amazed.

"He was living in my home with my family. I see that I'm going to be the big brother. I'm going to try and straighten out his character. He was giving me the business. He would be in and out of the bars and clubs. He would hitchhike, he would find his way, he would walk. I wanted to try and groom him. I'm out in the morning, getting gas. This guy says, 'Butch, we had a great time last night with that boxer, Leon Spinks. We took him out drinking.' I said, 'Whaaaat?'" Lewis spat out the words in disbelief. "Even during the Olympics, the team would run, and he would go maybe a block. He would go behind a clump of trees and lie down. He would splash water on his head, like he had been running."

Then Leon pulled off the biggest coup in boxing history, capturing the heavyweight championship from Muhammad Ali. Lewis said, "I took a kid with seven professional fights. Here we are upsetting a guy who carried boxing on his shoulders. When he pulled it off, Leon did it. He probably had more joy and happiness in his life. The fans accepted him beating Ali. They thought Leon was an everyday happy-go-lucky guy. He beat Ali. And we had the world by the balls."

Then it began to crumble. "The first thing he wanted was for me to give him some money to party," Lewis said. "'Leon,' I said, 'you can't go in some hole-in-the-wall places. You can't be seen in those juke joints.' Then he fell into the hands of these lawyers from Detroit. They flamboozled him. In the first fight, Leon made around $350,000. I wouldn't return all the money to him at once because I knew he would spend it. In the rematch, he made over $4 million."

Spinks and Ali fought a rematch seven month later but this time it was different. Lewis makes a pained face. "For the second fight, Leon was supposed to be at the arena at, let's say 7:00 P.M. Leon shows up at 9:15, 9:30, and the bout is at 10:00 P.M. " Lewis said. "He's got his entourage of Mr. T and his friends from Detroit. I have no idea of who these people are. They wouldn't even let his brother get near him. 'Leon,' I said, 'where were you? What is on your mind? You're fighting the heavyweight championship of the world!'

"We didn't know what was going to happen. These lawyers and handlers were thieves. I said, 'Leon, I'm through.' I was so enraged. They didn't even have his equipment. He fought in Mike Rossman's cup. That hundred-man entourage—they left his whole equipment bag behind! I went myself to borrow Mike Rossman's cup after he beat Galíndez. The cup was still wet. He didn't have *any* equipment. (He puts his head in his hands.) I can't express the feeling. I can't express my anger. That was it. That was it! I told Slim (his name for Michael) 'I want nothing to do with him. He can jump off the top of the Superdome.'

"He knows right and wrong. He says, 'Leave me alone. Let me do my own thing.' It's become a pattern.

"Then, against my better judgment, I got him a job at Ditka's in Chicago. Leon started drinking with his customers. It was getting pretty embarrassing.

"Leon has experienced the American Dream, and then it turned out to be the nightmare of a lifetime," Lewis said. "It was like trying to rush everything into a very short time. He threw his money away. He was ripped off. Everything he touched would go haywire.

"He means well—but another voice, like a cartoon devil, is always plucking the angel on his shoulder and says, 'Let's go.'"

Like Lewis, John Caluwaert thought he could assist Leon with his professional and personal affairs, but a similar pattern emerged. Caluwaert, a Chicago attorney, signed Leon Spinks to a managerial contract in 1991, managing him through eight fights—six wins and two losses. Leon's last fight was in February 1993; he lost a ten-round decision to an opponent who was 2–41. Caluwaert had met Leon at a party for one of his clients, and Leon expressed a desire for a comeback; Caluwaert needed to be sure of his intentions.

"I had a couple of psychologists meet with Leon for about six hours in this office—I wanted an unbiased standpoint," Caluwaert said. "They said that he was a man with a great heart, he had a belief in the kind of thing that we were trying to put together for him, and that he came from an extraordinary, difficult, tough background, an abusive background as a child. He found the gym as a means to show that he had talent, the ability to compete, and he showed that he could rise to the top."

Caluwaert put together an investment group which handled everything from transportation to purchasing Leon's robe and finding an apartment. "We gave him a weekly allowance, all advanced against purses," he said. "And we never made an effort to collect it."

Caluwaert thought it would be a challenge and that, in the right environment, Spinks would thrive and change. "I wanted him to build up his self-confidence himself, and one of my biggest mistakes was succeeding in doing that." Caluwaert sighed. "We were able to get him a driver's license, which was shortly lost based on a DUI (driving under the influence of alcohol) only a few months after we initiated our campaign. I think he allows himself to be overdependent on whoever may be there to offer help at the time. If you give him the vehicle and fill it with gas, he can steer it, but when it runs out of gas, he's looking for someone to refuel the tank. He seems to have been willing to settle for standards that are not necessarily defined by money; he seems to be content in living off his fame, and living day to day."

When Leon lost his license, Robell McMillar, Caluwaert's assistant, would pick him up every morning to take him to the gym and bring him back home. "Leon would show up, but then we would drop him off at the gym and go back to pick him up and not find him. He might be at a bar having a beer," Caluwaert said.

Caluwaert and his team took Leon through eight fights—he lost two—before they decided that he should retire. "I thought maybe I shouldn't let him fight anymore," Caluwaert said. "'Leon, I'm not sure we want to pursue this career any further. Maybe we can do other things—market memorabilia, maybe get you involved with community work,' and he said, 'No, I really want this.' I suggested to Leon that his greatness may be intact because he made his decision to quit when it was time, versus to have his greatness to be placed in mockery and give that shot to the press one more time. It doesn't penetrate because he doesn't see the big picture.

"What we experienced is that we're just one of those links in that chain. He's a unique optimist in that he believes every-thing will be okay. Period. I think he wakes up in the morning saying, 'I'll get through the day.'"

Caluwaert added, "If Leon gravitates to the position where he was when we first met him, I wouldn't be surprised to imagine the sound of coins dropping into a tin cup."

McMillar feels that Leon's wife, Betty, was a negative influ-ence. "Betty's attitude was that she wanted to be important more than Leon. His weakness is nagging. If they needed some food and she didn't want Leon to go to the gym, she would say 'Leon, we need to go shopping.' Leon couldn't stand the nagging. He's a lonely, scared type of man. He's the type of man who could not be by himself."

McMillar knew Leon for almost five years. "I don't think John [Caluwaert] was a sucker," he said. "We all lost a lot of money and a lot of effort. We were dreamers. But it was an experience. Leon was living in a bad environment: no lights, no gas, water shut off. The day John showed up was a day before they were going to put him in the street. I heard a lot of negative things about Leon. He was an older man, now, married. He got chil-dren and grandchildren. In my head, I say maturity needs anoth-er chance. It was an opportunity to do something positive. I said that I believed it can work if we all put our best efforts. I said, 'Leon, this is your last chance. You're pushing forty.'"

**LEON SPINKS—
World Heavyweight
Champion**

McMillar became close friends with Leon, and they used to drive around and talk. "Out of his family, he told me that he was the most mistreated," McMillar said. " 'Dinnertime would come,' he said, 'and my mother would give me the biggest piece of chicken. I found out it was the back with no meat.' We would talk and he would cry.

"Michael turned out perfect. Leon turned out not so perfect," McMillar added gravely. "I don't like the word 'pity.' I don't think it's his fault. Something happened in his life that messed up his mind. If you spend enough hours with him, you can influence him to do almost anything.

"They say in the Bible that God takes care of babes and fools. I believe that's what's going to happen to him."

Leon lives with his second wife, Betty, in a small town outside of Chicago. They met in 1980 at Archie's Cocktail Lounge in Detroit. "I didn't know who he was. I said, 'Are you Leon Spinks for real?'" she said. "I liked his kindness. He was nothing like people said. He was a big, cuddly teddy bear. He loved to laugh, loved to tell jokes, and," she added, "I liked tall mens anyway."

Leon, at forty-one, complains that when he works out in a gym, people take his false teeth. And, at a nearby restaurant, where he had lunch, a woman exclaims, "It's that boxer! Leon Spritz!" He laughs. "People see me and say, 'No, you're not Leon Spinks. Leon Spinks doesn't have no teeth.' People take my teeth. They do weird things—people are weird." He carries himself with the pomp of a former champion, but his face looks sullen and bored. Still, when he grins, he looks like that smiling Leon Spinks who won the heavyweight championship.

Even Spinks admits that he was not the best-trained athlete. "I tried to do some sneaky things to get by," he admitted. "I was in the service. No sense of me trying to go out and run. I was too tired to do anything. I might run at night when people didn't see me.

"When I beat Muhammad Ali, I went out and partied, I dance all night long. I was wild. My bodyguard had to carry me into the hotel, I was so tired.

"People call themselves my friends, pat you on the back. 'I'm from your hometown.' That's the way it was. Money got stolen from the lawyers. All my money that was invested was gone. I was scared to track the guy down in Detroit. My money went with him. I had $3.75 million. I'm a friendly guy. I would give you the shirt off my back. I try and do the best, and they stab me in the back and try and hurt me. I regret the way I was. People took advantage of me. I can't change nothing that I did. I had my goals, my dream, and I went for it. I tried to get what I could.

"I used cocaine, smoked a little pot, drank a little liquor, and went home," he admitted. "But never in training. On my free time. I'm an alcoholic because I can't handle alcohol.

"Michael was the pet. I'm the one getting the whipping. Michael was Mom's favorite. We had to clean the house. He got by with a lot of stuff. She used to beat me up all the time—she was staying in shape. Mom had her faults, but she didn't drive when she drank. And then I think she got religion. My father was alright. My mother didn't like the way he lived. She threw him out a long time ago. I was not older than six or seven. I was Leon Spinks, Jr. I would get my butt whipped because she didn't like him. She took a lot of stuff out on me. What kind of hell I was going through," he said, staring off into space. "She used the lamp cord and everything she could get her hands on. This went on for a long time. When I turned fifteen and got my first job and I got my first paycheck, my mom beat me to the mailbox. She gave me what she wanted. I left home. I was out on the streets. I was hustling, trying to keep some money in my pockets. I told Mom I was leaving—that was the tenth grade. I was grown.

"I'm not allowing people to take advantage of me now. I'm more aware of it. I got a big heart. Betty made me strong. She has a way of putting me in check. I feel sorry for people and I try and help them as much as I can. Some people take advantage of that.

"I think my dreams are my own. I still have my dreams. I must be doing something right. People are still talking about me."

For Bob Foster, the transition from champion to mortal was easier. He won the world light-heavyweight title back in 1968; Foster, always taller than most of his opponents, kept luring them in with his left hand, then setting them up with a right hand or left hook. He completely dominated the light heavy-

weight division and retired in 1978. Born and raised in Albuquerque, New Mexico, the father of four and grand-father of eleven retired again, this time as a deputy sheriff in December 1993, after spending twenty-two years with the Albuquerque Police Department. Foster patrolled the streets, investigated armed robberies as a detective, and escorted fugitives arrested on warrants. He joined the police department in 1971, seven years before he retired from box-ing. "I always did have a job," he said. "My mother always taught me—you always keep yourself a job. You got to learn to save."

Foster is repainting the outside of the house a bright blue, and has just added a front porch. He inspects for leaks, run-ning his hand over the damp windowsill. At fifty-six, he is still tall, trim, and rangy. His house is comfortable, filled with recliners, sofas, photos, and knickknacks.

"I enjoyed the sport of boxing," Foster said. "I just loved getting into the ring and outsmarting the next guy. I never val-ued money—$250,000 was good money for a championship fight in the sixties and seventies. This was before Top Rank, before TV. Some guys make so much money that it's tough for them to go back where they came from."

Alexis Argüello went right back to where he came from: Nicaragua. He never had trouble making weight; he was a fierce technician who would wait for his opponent to make a mistake. "I don't miss nothing. If I were born again, I would do the same thing." Argüello made his name against Aaron Pryor, first in 1982 and again the following year. "I never thought I would live through it. Pryor was twenty-seven, I was thirty-one—there was a big difference. I was the best on this earth," he recalled. Formerly a WBA featherweight and WBC super-featherweight champion and then the world lightweight champion, Argüello attempted to win his fourth title, the WBA junior welterweight, against Pryor, a tireless fighter with incredible stamina. Each round was hard fought. Pryor sat in his corner in the fourteenth round and drank from his water bottle, coming out when the bell rang as if it were the first round. The fight was stopped with Argüello on the canvas. Some thought there was an illegal substance in the water

BOB FOSTER— World Light- Heavyweight Champion

bottle; Pryor claimed that there wasn't. In their rematch in 1983, Argüello was knocked out in the tenth round, proving that Pryor's victory was no fluke. "He had the youth, strength, and speed that I didn't have anymore," Argüello said. He retired in 1986 after 86 bouts, after doctors discovered a heart condition. "When I had a heart problem, I realized it was over. It was hard. I called my kids and said 'I'm done.' I didn't have the desire or the conditioning. This is God's decision," he affirmed. "It has to happen sooner or later."

Argüello could have stayed in Miami, but he returned to Nicaragua to fight to get his houses and property back from the Sandinistas. A brother—one of Nicaragua's Freedom Fighters—was killed, and Argüello joined the battle briefly. He is now a champion of his people. Argüello travels between Nicaragua and Miami, where he owns a thirty-four-unit apartment building and a hardware store. "With Nicaragua, we're trying to fix the whole country. I don't want to be a politician— I tell my people, 'The day you see me as a politician, spit in my face.' I don't believe in guns." Argüello is rail thin, his eyes and his words weighty with passion. "The best way is to speak to

WILLIE PEP AND ALEXIS ARGÜELLO— World Featherweight Champion and Featherweight, Junior Lightweight, and World Lightweight Champion

the people. I go everywhere. The Sandinistas were supposed to set up a democratic system. President Violeta Chamorro—she's a nice lady who knows nothing about politics. She's being manipulated. I am just a man who loves my country and who wants Nicaraguans to live under one roof. Radio show, TV show, I have the tools to get to my people. The presidential elections are in 1996—I hope I'll be a part of it. I would love to an ambassador.

"I've been receiving death threats. Dying for my country is a blessing. I'm not afraid to die for my country. I expect it to happen. It's what we can do for the damn country. We need to take care of future generations," Argüello said fervently. "I've seen people who have gotten killed. I want to take the evil out of the country. In 1980 the Sandinistas took my farm, my houses, my cars, ninety acres of land, and a half a million dollars from the bank."

Argüello has given his boxing mementos to his friends. "It doesn't mean anything to me. I don't have anything but the belts," he said. The belts are in his home in Nicaragua. "Only to me, this means so much. The belts are worth twenty-five cents, but to me it's personal. I know what they mean."

Aaron Pryor, his former nemesis, rose, crashed, and burned. Pryor turned pro in 1976 and moved up quickly. In his first shot at the WBA junior welterweight title in 1980, he knocked out Antonio Cervantes. Pryor held his title through eight title defenses including his two victories over Argüello, until the end of 1983. In a dispute with his manager, Pryor announced his retirement and gave up his belt to break the contract. The International Boxing Federation (IBF) named him its champion a month later. He defended his title twice. Then eye problems—a complete tear of the retina in one eye and cataracts in both eyes—forced him to retire in 1985. He fought off and on until 1990, in states that somehow declared him fit to box.

Pryor can see you best if you stand back a few feet. His eyes drift to the side; his left eye squints when he is tired, and his voice trails off at the end of sentences. "When I wear the contact lens, my eye is back straight," said Pryor, thirty-nine. "I'm seeing bleary, yeah. I'll be able to see everything in front

**AARON PRYOR—
Junior Welterweight
Champion**

of me. I can see anything but the newspaper. I can see the whole newspaper without my contact; I just can't read it."

Although it would be difficult for him to obtain a license to box in the United States because of his eyesight, Pryor says that he is contemplating a comeback. "I would fight Chávez in Mexico or Camacho in Puerto Rico. I would come back for that. I'm not going to fight a two-dollar fight. For a million, a half a million, I would do it. Boxing is a part of you. When something is part of you, only Mother Nature can tell you what to do. It has to take its course. It's a combination of money and to see if I can do it. Larry Holmes, George Foreman, even Sugar Ray Leonard came back for a few. We have a bunch of idols doing it. I would take the chance. Eight states would license me. We're talking about different countries, fighting their hero. I retired undefeated. [No, he didn't; he lost to Bobby Joe Young in 1987.] I want to know how far I could have went."

"He had to retire because of drugs. He was drained, he was super drained," said Pryor's friend, the Reverend H. L. Harvey. "He had a mansion in Cincinnati, a house in Florida, vans, jeeps, trucks, cars. I asked him, 'Now what do you have? No one put a gun to your head.' When he went to the bank, everyone went to the bank. When he went to the crack houses, they went to the crack houses."

Reverend Harvey rescued Pryor from the hell of Liberty City, Miami, three years ago, risking his own life to save his friend's. Pryor, gaunt, his complexion the color of ashes, would wear the same clothes and the same glassy-eyed look for weeks. Reverend Harvey knocked on doors, homes, and crack houses, evading bullets and death threats. When he did manage to locate Pryor, "I went in one door, he went out another," he recalled. "They did not want him to leave because he had money. I'm taking money away from them. They would say, 'Here comes the Rev!' I was just like the police. Everyone on the street knew I was coming." One night Reverend Harvey put Pryor to bed in Pryor's home in Miami. "People were ringing the doorbell shouting, 'Nigger, come out! We're going to kill you!'"he said. Pryor was snoring, Harvey trembling. Eventually, Pryor's house, along with his other possessions, was repossessed.

Harvey made his mind up that he wouldn't leave Pryor behind. But Pryor would cash in tickets left for him and buy crack with the money. "I tricked him," Harvey recalled. "I put him in the car. The plane was leaving at 7:00 P.M. I told him it was seven in the morning. We drove to the airport, and I told him, 'We're going to meet someone,' and we got on the plane. But he went back. The amount of drugs he was doing, anyone else would have been dead. Someone once sold him a real rock instead of crack. He went through two million dollars."

After several trips to Miami, Reverend Harvey finally succeeded. "I saw some good in him," he said. "I refused to give up on him. I wasn't going to let him go. We were real close friends; I was like his spiritual father. He donated a couple of pews to the church—you never forget what people do for you. When he was down, no one was there. I had to go to his rescue."

Pryor finally gave up crack. "I had to hold him all night when he was trying to withdraw this poison," Harvey said quietly. "The last time, he went cold turkey."

Pryor recalled, "I was doing crack and cocaine—that was enough. I was truly infected. I started back in 1986, 1987. My wife was divorcing me; I would get clean physically but not mentally," Pryor explained. "At one time, I didn't want to listen. Some people hoped that I would go back out in the streets. For others, I was their idol and inspiration. I was feeling that all of my life I wanted to be the champion. Dr. [Frank] Doggett said that I shouldn't fight in Atlantic City before I got my eye fixed. I became very depressed. They took my title. I had to look for a scapegoat. It took over a year to do that. I worked very hard to be the best, and they took my title. I was so depressed. Then my wife left me. She still lives in Florida. I don't know what her situation is. I gave up on me. I realized I was hurting people. I let go and found God. I just quit. I went to two drug programs. I came back out. I wasn't ready. I decided to go cold turkey. Now, when I get the urge, I pray.

"Any chemical that you put in your body affects your system. Who knows about it?" He shrugged. "I've been clean a year and a half. I stopped being stubborn. With drugs, you can be an actor, you can be a thief. People told me, 'We don't want you to hurt yourself.' I was a public person. I blew at least a couple of hundred thousand. I had a lot of money stolen from me. People forged bad checks and power of attorney, people took advantage of me."

Pryor says that he has been clean for the last two years. He still lives in Cincinnati, this time with his girlfriend, Frankie, who keeps a watchful eye on him, and he lives off the interest of some money he had put away. His complexion is clear, his handshake firm. His stomach protrudes a little over the waistline of his pants. And when he trains young fighters at several different gyms, his demeanor is that of a friendly, professional, and captivating instructor. Many do not know who he is.

A gaggle of kids, from four to twenty-four, swarm over him **AARON PRYOR** as he leads the group in drills, army style, and when the littlest one comes over for help after he has worked with a profession-al, Pryor puts on the mitts again and starts over. "I felt by being a fighter for twenty-five years, I could be more helpful in the community and in boxing than anywhere else. I'd love to start with professional fighters in Vegas and New York," he lament-ed, thoughts of a comeback pushed aside for the moment.

Ken Norton, on a comeback from a devastating car accident in February 1986, is still muscular, but he walks with a slight limp and wears a baseball cap to cover the scars. "I'm involved in a company that sells and installs telephone systems, com-puters, and faxes," he said, signing a pair of tiny boxing gloves. "I'm involved in car and alarm systems, and I own a health club."

Norton fought Ali three times. He beat Ali in 1973 and broke his jaw for the North American Boxing Federation (NABF) heavyweight title; and then lost twice, the second fight a split decision, the third time by a controversial unanimous decision at Yankee Stadium. Norton was hard to hit because he came at Ali with a crablike defense and could defuse Ali's punches.

"I admire the man as a showman and as an athlete. If it wasn't for any Ali, there would be no Ken Norton," he said respectfully. "With Ali there was no animosity. There was a mutual respect. I know after the accident, he was one of the first people visiting the hospital. He didn't have to come. He's a very good man."

Norton was awarded the opportunity to fight for the WBC heavyweight title after he beat Jimmy Young in 1977 but Leon Spinks, the current titleholder, chose to fight Ali instead of him. The WBC then stripped Leon of his title and gave it to Norton, who lost it on his first defense to Larry Holmes in 1978. The aggressive Norton threw an assortment of punches. He was big and muscular, but Holmes's jab won him the fight.

"I don't miss it at all." Norton turned to hug a small boy who poked him timidly for his autograph. "I don't miss getting up to box. I didn't start boxing until I was twenty-five or twenty-six. I wanted to go to school first. I went to two and a half years of college to study elementary education. I couldn't be locked up in a school, teaching. Boxing just happened. I miss the people, the fans, the press. I miss that aura. I don't miss boxing. I didn't want to sacrifice anymore," he said simply. "Regrets? That I didn't really train as hard as I could. Rather than being obsessed, I was just competing. I wasn't obsessed by it. Ali, Frazier, Bob Foster—they were obsessed by it. I was an athlete. I enjoyed being one of the best."

If it weren't for Joe Frazier, Muhammad Ali would not have achieved the same greatness as a fighter. But Frazier suffered. "His words hurt me, me and my family. He called me a gorilla, the white man's champion, telling me that I was stupid. Why did he have to say this?" Frazier asks no one in particular. "If he were fighting today, I'd fight him."

"Vietnam, it was not my place. I'm not about war, I'm not a politician. I'm a world champion. My job is boxing. Once you

KEN NORTON—
Heavyweight
Champion

start overstepping your job, then you'll get into trouble."

"*I* wasn't stripped of my title. *I* could do what I wanted. *He* was Muhammad Ali. He might have been greater if it weren't for me. I slowed his clock. I love Muhammad. I have a lot of respect for the man. Parkinson's?—*I* didn't have anything to do with it."

"If my father could fight Ali today, he would go at it," says his eldest daughter, Jacquelyn Frazier-Lyde, an attorney who works out of the same North Philadelphia gym-cum-office that her father owns. "Because my father really befriended him, my father helped Ali get his license back (after Ali was stripped of his title for refusing to take part in the military draft), he loaned him money . . . it really shocked him. He was completely betrayed."

Jacqui, who was thirteen at the time of the 1975 "Thrilla in Manila," remembers, "People went for what Ali was saying about my father. They thought my father was ignorant. My father is a very loyal person. He didn't say anything. All he could do was focus on fighting. He was completely shocked and betrayed, and he had to go through it publicly."

Frazier's elder son, Marvis, who was fourteen at the time, accompanied his father to the Philippines for the bout. "I was upset and confused," he recalls. "This guy [Ali] was supposed to be a black leader; he was supposed to be for brotherhood and for God. But God didn't go out and call people names. Pop was the everyday workingman, always humble. The other guy had the lip. Ali, being a black man—maybe he had an identity crisis. My father didn't have to prove that he was black. Pop is very intelligent. People didn't take the time to listen. A lot of people fell into Ali's interpretation. No one has taken the time—'Joe, what about this? What's your view?'

"Kids would draw little stick figures," Marvis remembers. "The stick figure with his hands up was Ali, and the figure on the ground was my father."

Marvis, whose own short-lived boxing career was highlighted by a thirty-second knockout at the hands of Mike Tyson, now manages the gym, organizes the annual Frazier Golden Gloves tournament, trains fighters, sets up personal appearances for his father, and does an uncanny imitation of Howard Cosell interviewing his father and Ali. Marvis says

**MUHAMMAD ALI—
World Heavyweight
Champion**

that he sees Ali as "a great person. The way he treated my dad, you forgive and forget." Still, he says, "He hurt us a lot, but what can I say? He did a lot for boxing. To me, he and my father made each other. If there had been no Ali, there would have been no Frazier, and vice versa."

Smokin' Joe, in his pink and white trunks and a sparkly green cornerman's jacket, still hops briskly into the ring to train fighters at his gym. It's been thirteen years since he retired in 1981. He has owned a restaurant and become a sporadic lounge singer (he still sings). He acts a little, including a voice-over for *The Simpsons*, trains fighters (he trained Marvis), and attends fights in the Philadelphia-Atlantic City areas, offering a few words and a handshake all around. Frazier is difficult to pin down, even though he lives above the gym in his bachelor "penthouse" (he and his wife Florence are separated), one floor above the gutted second floor, where he and his family are preparing the Frazier Community Center in the decayed North Philadelphia area.

"This gym," Frazier says, looking at the large framed photographs of himself mounted on the brick walls of the gym. "Something to give the black boys in the neighborhood, to get something out of life." When a crusty old fighter stumbles into the gym, it is Frazier who hands him a few dollars and some clothes. Marvis said that his father will never end up like that. "Pop?" He shook his head. "No way. He'll come live with us."

"I'm a man who's been through ups and downs with obstacles like hatred and bitterness," Joe Frazier says. He says that with money invested and a pension fund set up, he's financially secure. "See?" he points out. "Ordinary Joe ain't so ordinary."

He looks up at the photographs of himself on the wall and back down at himself, thicker around the middle, thinner at the top, and his dark eyes still guarded and wary. It is thirty-three years since he first fought Ali, also heavier and thinner at the top, whose movements and speech are slowed by Parkinson's, but whose mind and wit are still nimble. Frazier says of his former tormentor: "*I* ain't got Parkinson's. Why? I don't know. It's God's way. They beat me up. George [Foreman] beat me up. I'm fifty, and I ain't got nothing wrong with me. Case closed."

JOE FRAZIER—
World Heavyweight
Champion

151

Perhaps now Joe Frazier has his final victory over Ali at last. "Everything works. My mind's together," he bragged. "I don't have nothing to do with it," he said. "He can't blame me."

Earnie Shavers, a man with one punch—a devastating right hand—fought Ali and Holmes for the heavyweight title and lost. Today Shavers has a parcel full of complimentary letters from schools, prison wardens, and hospitals, speaking of God and the dangers of drugs. He has been a guest speaker at over fifty prisons and he has been interviewed by a prison newspaper. The headline reads "Earnie Shavers: Mugged by God" and recounts how he had lost his mansion, his Rolls-Royce, and his coast-to-coast network of girlfriends, blaming it on fast-talking promoters.

Shavers is both an evangelist and the author of the book *Choosing and Loving Your Wife God's Way.* In the book, he offers such advice as:

> Do not be yoked with an unbeliever.
> Don't marry a grouch!
> Be aware that she may not change.
> Husbands, please listen to what your wife has to say.
>> If you do, you will have far fewer headaches.
>> Believe me.
> Men, do you remember what first attracted your wife to
>> you? Those things should be guarded and improved.
> Men, it is sad to see a husband who has become careless
>> about his weight after the dating years are over.
> Your wife is not your opponent; compromises are
>> necessary.

The book posts a telephone number and address where you can contact Shavers with your testimonial or prayer request. There is also a form addressed, "To My Wife," a signed declaration of three items that "with God's wisdom and strength, I will change about myself."

Shavers now lives in Phoenix with his fourth wife, Cindy, and her two daughters. He lost everything in 1980, blaming it on his lifestyle. "I was rich and famous, I had a mansion—a thirteen-bedroom house with a mile-long driveway—limousines, and women, and I lost everything by living in the fast lane. The

bank foreclosed on the house, and I had to pay the IRS. But it allowed me to get my life in order. Money couldn't be my God."

Now, at fifty, Shavers is very much the salesman, selling long-distance telephone services and burglary prevention equipment. He plans to buy a Rolls-Royce for himself, a Mercedes for his wife, and a mansion for his family. Earnie Shavers Ministries can receive 10 percent of your telephone bill if you sign up for the telephone services, and Earnie Shavers Ministries—comprised of Earnie Shavers—speaks to youth groups in Phoenix when he is in town. Wearing a bright blue sweatsuit, he is bald and rotund, his cheeks rounder, but he walks lightly, like the former athlete that he once was.

"I listened to advice of older people. You guys, now is the time," he implored two teenage boys. "Don't procrastinate. By twenty-one, you could be dead or in jail. Stay in school. Keep it

EARNIE SHAVERS—
Heavyweight
Contender

up, man. Before you know it, you'll be an adult. Don't get an education—*boom!*—then you'll have no choices. I learned to ask questions and listen. You keep procrastinating, and look what happens—you're thirteen, fourteen, seventeen, eighteen, twenty-nine, then fifty and fifty-nine, you'll have nothing.

"The fight game opened a lot of doors for me," he said. "Now I can do anything I want to do. I talk in prisons, to gang members, inner-city youth. I travel all over the country. I'm not taking one dime. If I can get one young man or young lady to turn their life around, that'll be great.

"I can retire a millionaire today and live a million-dollar lifestyle. What I did years ago pays. I can go out and live my life. I care about you," he said, his eyes appearing moist. "I guarantee that it will change your whole life. I promise to come back to see how you're doing. All we want is for you to do your part."

The two young men listened, spellbound.

"Prisoners always tell me, 'Get to the young men. We don't want them in here,'" he continued. "They don't want to be in here. Get to the young people.

"Start preparing yourself. I came from a very small community of about five hundred people. I wanted to be a star athlete. They said that your chance of making it is like one in a million. I made it. I was twenty-one. I dreamed about being an athlete. I trained night and day, and it does not hurt you to dream. Dream big. You work, study, study people, yourself. Get an education. Don't let anyone tell you that you can't make it, or *you'll never make it!!"*

Shavers said that he is "putting together a gym on Seventh Street. I will come in on occasion," he promised. "I'm going to direct." He offered free uniforms and "doctor service," warning, "You have to prove yourself. Street fights are no good. Just walk away from it. You'll get hurt. You have nothing to prove to anyone. It's not worth it. You never lose your temper. Ali would psyche out his guys, and then they would get angry and make mistakes.

"When you're fighting, you're a piece of meat. You have to look out for yourself."

Eddie Gregg was a heavyweight with a college diploma who rose as high as number-three in the rankings; and when he traded in handshakes for toiling over paperwork under a fluorescent light bulb, he did so swiftly and with a sigh of relief. Tony Zale, the former middleweight champion, often says, "Boxing is the only sport that didn't go to college." But, just after he retired, Gregg combined his degree in sociology and torturous boxing experiences into a career counseling teenagers on occupations, education, drugs, birth control, long division, grammar, and the particulars and politics of survival. After Gregg retired, he never languished in the gym in the afterglow of his status as a contender and never became obsessed by what his future might have been. He was raised in an orphanage, took Don King to court and won but found himself blackballed. He's now forty-one and his eyes are old and mournful. "I've had money, I've been broke. I don't fear the crowds," he said quietly. "I fear the social implications of life. That's why I can relate to these kids."

Listening to Jake LaMotta is watching Jake LaMotta doing Robert DeNiro doing Jack LaMotta. "I do personal appearances, stand-up comedy. I do mostly sporting events, like baseball-card shows, wherever I get a job," he said. He has been married six times and has six children. The subject of *Raging Bull* in 1980, at the end he was a bloated comedian with stale jokes. "My popularity started to diminish. People didn't recognize me. The movie made me champ all over again," he said proudly. He still tells the jokes. "I talk about Rocky Graziano, about my wives. Hey, listen to these.

"My wife closes her eyes when we're making love. She hates to see me having a good time.

"Do you know what it means to go home to a woman who gives you warmth and tenderness? It means you're in the wrong goddamn apartment!

"I was so much in demand. No one wanted to fight me. I fought Sugar Ray Robinson six times. I fought him so many times that it's a wonder I don't have diabetes."

He stuck a cigar in the middle of his sad clown face and puffed away. "I'm the only one left in my era that people know—Rocky Graziano, Marcel Cerdan, Sugar Ray Robinson," he said. "I feel very lucky to be here. Pep was a great fighter and he's from my era, but he's not well known. So is Joey

**JAKE LaMOTTA—
World Middleweight
Champion**

Maxim, but he's not well known. If I were fighting Sugar Ray Robinson today, I would have gotten $25 million."

They say the only one tougher than Emile Griffith is his mother, known as "Mommy," a title of warm respect, to friends, acquaintances, his opponents, and the fighters he trains. Slightly stooped in a white polyester dress with bright flowers, white crew socks, sensible brown shoes, pearl earrings and a large wooden cane, seventy-one-year-old Emelda Griffith possesses a sharp eye, a sharp tongue, an unwavering devotion to her oldest son, and a purse that resembles a suitcase.

She wanted him to be a baseball player, not a prizefighter. Griffith, the five-time world welterweight and middleweight champion, born in the Virgin Islands fifty-six years ago and who still speaks with the island lilt, was employed as a shipping clerk at Albert's Millinery in Manhattan's garment district, when Howie Albert and his father, Pop Albert, noticed his muscular shoulders, tapered waist, and fast hands, and convinced him to enter the Golden Gloves. Mrs. Griffith was against it—her brother and late husband had boxed—so his sister Gloria signed the papers, moving his birthday back a year to reach the required eighteen. "I was crazy," she said. "I didn't want him to go." After he won the Golden Gloves in 1958, her husband, Emile Sr., died after suffering a stroke, and it was Emile Jr.'s purses that supported her and her eight children.

"I learned to like it," she said. "I knew that once he got in there, he could defend himself. The whole family traveled with him. I always told him before the fight, 'May God guide your hands to victory.'"

Those hands were victorious and in one sad, tragic moment, they were deadly. Griffith fought 112 fights from the late 1950s until he retired in 1977. A boxer, a little bit of a puncher, and an excellent counterpuncher, he was well trained by Gil Clancy and was well respected with a big New York following. Mrs. Griffith was a colorful, exuberant supporter, cheering him on from ringside and wearing one of the large, fancy hats he made for her. Afterward, Griffith extended his hand, a sandwich, and a few dol'ars to the less fortunate. "Those bums outside would really get to me," he recalled. "But before I would give them money, I'd say 'Let's go get something to eat first. Then here's $10, $25—do what you want to do." He had left high school in the twelfth grade, ashamed of his torn pants, so he would duck out and go someplace else. The big purses of the heavyweights missed his weight divisions; he said the most that he earned was $250,000 for one of three fights with Nino Benvenuti in the late 1960s. He purchased their five-bedroom home in Hollis, Queens, with cash from that purse.

Mrs. Griffith cooked him breakfast, bought him steak, washed and ironed his gym clothing, and pushed him out the door in the mornings. "She saw that I was really that serious, she gave me that extra push. When it was snowing outside, she would make me go out and run. And I did," he said. "I don't know where I would be without her."

When Griffith won the welterweight title from Benny Paret in Miami Beach in 1961, his mother had to be revived after jumping into the ring and fainting in her son's corner from the excitement.

"I got excited, not scared," Mrs. Griffith said. "Only one time—the accident in the ring." She hugged herself tighter and rocked back and forth gently. "I was so scared for both of them," she whispered. "That was terrible. When the threatening phone calls came, I had to send him away by night to the Virgin Islands. He didn't want to hurt nobody. It bothers him, still."

Paret, a sugarcane cutter from Cuba, had regained his title from Griffith five months later. In March 1962, Griffith became welterweight champion again by knocking out Paret in the twelfth round. Carried out of the ring unconscious, Paret died ten days later.

"It's still news," Griffith said tersely, looking away. "I don't like it. It took enough out of my life; it drained me. Sometimes I got angry with myself. I fought him, but Gene Fullmer started the damage, and they blamed me. But I was the last one to fight him. I was very scared."

Griffith retired in 1977, knowing that it was the end when he was knocked down in the first round, and he became a freelance trainer. He traveled between Gleason's Gym and the Times Square Gym to train fighters, hollering boisterously, intimidating to the naïve and reassuring to the rest. His estranged wife, Sadie, and their daughter live in the Virgin Islands; Griffith has lived with his mother for the last five years. A man more comfortable checking his watch and grumbling at a bus stop than sliding across the polished leather seat of a limousine, he is at ease in bars with last year's Christmas lights still up and with the camaraderie of shoe salesmen and deliverymen.

Perhaps it was for the $800 he was carrying; Griffith said that he doesn't remember what happened, but he was beaten and beaten badly at the end of July 1992 and almost died. He had just flown back from Australia with the former feather-

EMILE GRIFFITH— World Welterweight and Middleweight Champion

weight champion Juan LaPorte, who had lost a ten-round decision, and he stopped off at a bar in the Times Square area, set
his bags down, and began buying drinks with $50 bills.

"They tried to kill me!" he told his mother as he staggered
through the door that Sunday morning, his face swollen, the
skin raked off of one hand, his collarbone fractured, and his body
bruised and battered, his kidneys barely functioning. "He could
hardly move," his mother said. "It was like he was paralyzed."
He spent several months in the hospital. Griffith's younger sister, Karen, an ordained minister at Faith Baptist Church in
Queens, recited prayers daily as his mother held his hands.

"That I don't know," Griffith said of the attack. "I was
drinking in the bar. I think I got mugged. I got it good," he said
ruefully. "From now on, it's hello, good-bye, and no drinking or
smoking. I was scared, very scared."

Rough and unpolished, with a strong, snaky left jab, Sandy
Saddler fought 93 times before he knocked out Willie Pep with
a left hook in the fourth round to collect Pep's world featherweight title in 1948. He held two titles simultaneously, winning the junior lightweight title the following year. Saddler
and Pep met four times through 1951 in the roughest bouts in
boxing history, with Pep winning only once, flying furiously all
over Saddler to reclaim his title in a fifteen-round decision in
1949. Always a difficult target, Pep, clever and agile, bobbing
and weaving, dislocated his shoulder and lost his title at the
end of the seventh round of their third meeting when his arm
became hooked on Saddler's shoulder and he could not continue. In their last meeting, at the Polo Grounds, they
thumbed, fouled, butted, and wrestled each other to the
ground, with Saddler opening a deep cut over Pep's right eye
in the second round and dropping him with a left. Pep got back
on his feet and felled Saddler with a right to the jaw. He hit
him thirteen straight times without Saddler returning a punch.
But Pep surrendered, unable to leave his corner for the tenth
round, his right eye bruised and his body and ego battered.
Saddler was suspended, Pep's license revoked.

Saddler was inducted into the Army in 1952 and continued
to box after his honorable discharge in 1954. Injuries from a car
accident in 1956 left him blind in one eye, and he vacated his

title on the advice of his doctor. At thirty, he had fought 162 fights and knocked out 103 men in twelve years.

Like some older people, Saddler, who is sixty-eight, sometimes forgets names, dates, and places, where he lives and how old he is. "I'm fifty-five," he declared. He said he enjoys living in his hotel very much and how beautiful it is. He put on his cap and his coat and says he's heading for the gym. "Gotta go to the gym and work out," he said. "Gotta go hit that bag, do my roadwork. Yes, sir."

Saddler lives in a nursing home in the Bronx with copies of his ring record and of a photograph of a young, baby-faced Saddler taped to the wall. His name is taped to his locker, as it used to be in the gym.

He remembers his fights—maybe not all 162 of them, which is a lot for a man to remember—but mention Willie Pep, and Saddler starts showing off his jab. And shadowboxing.

"Boy, them fights was something!" Saddler smiled to himself and closed his eyes. "I just looked at him, and he just looked at me, and when the bell rang—boy, would we both go at it! I knew good and well how he fought. I was good out there, and I took it away from him. He was always a pretty good fighter, a pretty good puncher. I knew all the different moves that he had and I was ready. He was a show-off, and I knew everything that he had."

But Saddler's paydays never matched his potential. He earned $100 or so per fight, he said, and he took home maybe $10,000 for each of the Pep fights. "He was cheated out of a lot of money," said trainer Ray Arcel. "He never reaped the rewards. If you didn't watch yourself, they'd take the eyes out of your head. There were more thieves in Stillman's Gym than in the penitentiary."

After he retired, Saddler worked as the athletic director of the National Maritime Union, offering boxing and athletic instruction to merchant seaman until several years ago, when the building was sold. He also trained promising young amateur fighters at Gleason's on 30th Street.

"He loved working with those kids," said his longtime friend Amelia Acey. "He used to take them all out to eat after the fights. Sandy would run every evening," she remembered. "He never was a womanizer. He never stayed

out late at night; he never drank; he never smoked. He was beautiful," she sighed deeply and sadly. "He called me every night. He was thoughtful, a very quiet and shy person, very humble."

"Sandy, you're a dead man," was carved into Saddler's apartment door at 151st and Edgecombe Avenue when Danny Kapilow found him five years ago, after noticing his absence at a boxing dinner. Estranged from the wife he said he married while in the Army and their two grown children, Saddler lived alone. He was afraid to open the door. "People came around asking for money all night," Acey said. "They'd follow him into the building and rob him. Checks were stolen out of his mailbox. He was attacked and hit on the head with an iron pipe. His apartment was ransacked."

"I saw the squalor and the fear," Kapilow said. "We had to get him out."

Kapilow, a welterweight contender of the 1940s, mobilized his organization, Ring 8, a brotherhood of boxers that looks after the welfare of veteran fighters in New York City, to move Saddler to another apartment.

Not long after, Saddler was found by the police wandering through Brooklyn late at night, robbed of his wallet and his eyeglasses. Kapilow, Arcel, Acey, and Tino Raino, another ex-fighter, arranged for him to be placed in a nursing home.

"Gotta do my roadwork," Saddler said, shadowboxing.

His son said earlier that his father's bouts with forgetfulness are part of the aging process. Acey, who has known Saddler since 1979, is uncertain. "He deteriorated just like that. But up until that time, he was a strong, healthy man. There are boxers who took more blows than Sandy. I knew it was something more than that."

"Who do you think you're kidding?" Kapilow retorted. "Head punches cause brain damage. He had over 200 amateur fights and over 160 professional fights. They kept him churning like a money machine," he said bitterly. "You can imagine what they made from this kid. We were in the gym together, and he was always the sweetest, most polite young man you'd ever see. But what can you do? This happened to all of us. If you made a beef, that would be your last fight. Sandy would never try and get answers."

SANDY SADDLER—
World Featherweight
and Junior
Lightweight
Champion

"Well, I wish him the very best luck in the world," said Willie Pep, not unkindly. "He ain't going to get any better, but I hope he's well. Tell him to keep punching. He was a helluva fighter."

Chuck Wepner is not sentimental. He has sold his robes, boxing gloves, and shoes, and sold or given away plaques and trophies. "I'd rather get the money and enjoy it now," he said. "If I die right now, someone will say, 'So what do we do with all this stuff?'"

At fifty-four, Wepner has a wife named Theresa, two ex-wives, a calico cat, and a waistline just an inch over what it used to be. A tough fighter who never blocked or ducked a punch in his career, he says that he has changed since his fighting days. "I've mellowed," he said, straightening a plaque on the wall. "Years ago, I used to go out and party, with the women, the jewelry, the cars. I was making $70–80,000 back then. I got tired of running around. I was ready to settle down."

Wepner sells eggs and liquor, makes appearances, and does a little public relations and sales for a steel-drum company. He vacuums when his wife is at work. Wepner never left Bayonne. He lives across from Veteran's Stadium, where he made his pro debut in 1964, stopping Lightning George Cooper in the third round on what is now the pitcher's mound.

"I used to love to go to the gym," he said. "I never had a lot of talent. I was not a great puncher or boxer. My M.O. was conditioning, wearing my opponents down and catching up with them later on. I started cheating a little bit with my training at the end. I didn't like it anymore. I look at the champ [Ali]. The poor guy," he said. "It was all that rope-a-dope crap. I retired in 1978. If I hadn't fought Muhammad Ali, people wouldn't remember me. I always gave 100 percent."

In 1988 Wepner was charged with possession, conspiracy, and distributing cocaine. He said, "I regret doing time in prison. I regret that. Right after I retired in 1978, I didn't miss the actual fighting, I missed the adulation. So I started looking for something different. Then I got myself in trouble. They offered me a deal, and I told them to go fuck themselves. I'm not a rat. I hate rats. Years ago, there was an honor, a code. Not anymore. They sentenced me to ten years. I did three. I kept my mouth shut. People gave me a second chance."

CHUCK WEPNER—
Heavyweight
Contender

David "Poison" Kotei, who could box and punch, was Ghana's first world champion; he won the WBC featherweight title with a fifteen-round decision over Rubén Olivares in 1975. Kotei lost his title in Accra the following year, to Danny López. "It was a great shock," he said. "The whole nation was crying. It was a national defeat." Kotei's house is dusty. His furniture, of fine quality two decades ago, looks worn and tired. His bed sags. Old newspapers and magazines are scattered about. Kotei said that he had started a fishing business, but abandoned that enterprise when his old wooden canoe developed leaks.

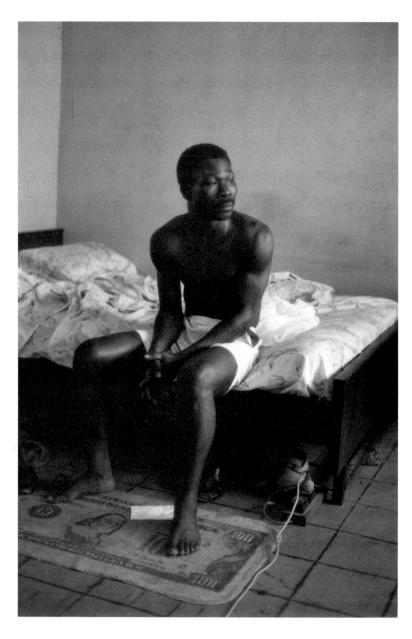

**DAVID KOTEI—
Featherweight
Champion**

When José Torres became the first world champion from Puerto Rico, the popular light heavyweight was regaled through New York's Spanish Harlem on the evening of his defeat of Willie Pastrano back in 1965. A man bellowing into a bullhorn noted his arrival and thousands of people blocked off the streets near 110th Street and Lexington Avenue to get a glimpse of him. *"Chegüi! Chegüi!"* they shouted. *"El campeón!"* He was raised to a second-floor fire escape where he addressed his people.

**JOSÉ TORRES—
World Light-
Heavyweight
Champion**

JACKIE "KID"
BERG—World Junior
Welterweight
Champion

Twenty-nine years later, he went back to the same street to pose for photographs in his old robes and trunks. At fifty-eight, he is grayer and squarely built; the robe could not hide the cloak of age. Some of the older men who still lived in the neighborhood recognized him and greeted him with a handshake and *"Chegüi! El campeón!"* And for those too young to know who he was or who needed an explanation, he was simply "Mr. Torres." The neighborhood is poorer and the corner of 110th and Lexington is now a favored spot for drug addicts and dealers. A few gathered under the fire escape where he recreated his scene and they yelled again. Cars slowed down and drivers peered through the passenger side to see what was happening. A crowd gathered for autographs, drawing dollar bills out of their wallets for his signature in a neighborhood where a life is often worth much less. He signed and shook hands and posed for photographs in the local meat market. "You know," he said afterward, "it all started coming back to me again!"

Many prizefighters reclaim their fame in a town smaller than Kotei's Accra. Canastota, New York, twenty miles east of Syracuse, is a town of 5,000 where you're born, where you reside, and where, before you die, a dinner is thrown in your honor. Split by the Erie Canal and with an airstrip from which Amelia Earhart took off and landed, it is the home of the two world champions: Carmen Basilio, who was known as the Onion

KID GAVILÁN—
World Welterweight
Champion

**LOU AMBERS—
World Lightweight
Champion**

Farmer because he once worked picking onions in the muck (he hates onions), and his nephew, Billy Backus. They both held the world welterweight title; Basilio was also a world middleweight champion in the 1950s.

Canastota is also the home of the International Boxing Hall of Fame, whose annual induction ceremonies draw current and retired fighters, trainers, managers, collectors, and fans. Beau Jack, world lightweight champion, Jackie "Kid" Berg, a world junior welterweight champion, and Lou Ambers, also a world lightweight champion, are among the inductees. It is a place where heroes and idols gather; old champions meet newer ones; champions and contenders meet their opponents, sometimes for only the second time; where trainers and champions are reunited, and where old rivalries are not forgotten. Buddy McGirt met Archie Moore, Vinnie Pazienza embraced his hero, Willie Pep; Ray Arcel greeted Tony Zale warmly; Earnie Shavers met Ken Norton; Willie Pep shook hands with Sandy Saddler and shared a laugh with Alexis Argüello; Muhammad Ali hugged George Chuvalo; Archie Moore chatted with Bob Foster; Michael Spinks was reunited with Eddie Futch; Bobby Czyz picked up a few pointers from Don Dunphy, and Joey Giardello and Gene Fullmer, two old opponents with grudges, avoided each other.

At the Hall of Fame's collectors' show, which resembles a large flea market, an autographed photograph of Sylvester

**BEAU JACK—
World Lightweight
Champion**

Stallone sells for $50, $35 more than Joe Frazier's. Muhammad Ali's father's driver's license sells for $300, while Tyson has become immortalized as a plastic doll complete with prison stripes and gold tooth for $25. A baseball-style card of Emile Griffith is worth $1; Ken Norton and Marvin Hagler $2 apiece. Buddy McGirt purchased a photograph of his idol, Archie Moore, for $35; a McGirt photograph sells for $8.

"I don't feel bad," said Moore, who retired in 1963 at the age of fifty, after twenty-seven years and 229 bouts; he was light heavyweight champion of the world for ten years. "I'm waiting for someone to break that record so that I can start a comeback," he said lightly. He says that he is eighty, but his family has figured out that he is somewhere between seventy-nine and eighty-five—he's changed it so much that even he's forgotten. "As time marches on, so do events. You have to step aside and help others who are coming up. This is fate. Time flies, boy, it flies," he said mournfully. He shook his head; his hand curled itself into a fist.

"I'd sure like to fight," he added, sounding wistful. "Father Time—him you can't beat."

INDEX

Lewis, Butch (manager), 126, 129, 130, 131
Lewis, Ted (Kid), 99
Liston, Sonny, 100, 103
Lpez, Danny, 165
Louis, Joe, 33, 90, 99
   in retirement, 119, 121

Mamby, Saoul, 34
Mancini, Ray, 20, 122, 123 *illus.*
Marciano, Rocky, 26, 27 *illus.*, 34, 90
Marcus, Egerton, 46
Marotta, Ace (trainer), 99
Maxim, Joey, 34
McClellan, Gerald, 31
McGirt, Buddy, 55, 56 *illus.*, 56, 77
McGuigan, Barry, 121
McLaglen, Victor, 122
Medal, Mark, 74
Menefee, Tony, 113, 114, 117
Molinares, Toms, 53
Monzón, Carlos, 53, 122
Moore, Archie, 19, 23, 54, 55 *illus.*, 100, 121, 172
Moore, Davey, 112
Morrison, Tommy, 29, 59, 60 *illus.*, 84
Muhammad, Eddie Mustafa, 121

Nelson, Azumah, 64 *illus.*, 65-66
Nieves, Pete, 82 *illus.*
North American Boxing Federation (NABF), 147
Norton, Ken, 32, 145, 146 *illus.*, 147

O'Grady, Sean, 121
Olajide, Jr., Michael, 122
Olivares, Rubn, 165
Ortz, Carlos, 96, 106

Paret, Benny, 158
Pastrano, Willie, 35, 53, 166
Patterson, Floyd, 29, 121
Pazienza, Vinnie, 171
Pedroza, Eusebio, 34
Pep, Willie, 90, 100, 121, 140 *illus.*, 160, 171
Plimpton, George, 19
prizefighters, 16 *illus.*. See also boxers
   frequency of bouts, 77-78
   as heroes, 54
   as managers and trainers, 121
   movie roles of, 122

   in prison, 122
   race/ethnicity of, 17, 28, 83-84
   regimen of, 31
   relationship with trainers, 31-33
   in retirement, 119-126
   reunion of old fighters, 171
   short careers of, 125
prize money, 76-78, 80, 126
promoters, 70
Pryor, Aaron, 96, 141-145, 142 *illus.*, 145
   illus.

Raging Bull (film), 155
Raino, Tony, 163
Randolph, Leo, 121
Robinson, Sugar Ray, 53, 90, 93, 122
Rodrguez, Tiny, 28
Rome Boxing Club, 51 *illus.*
Rosario, Edwin, 38 *illus.*
Rosenbloom, Maxie, 121, 122
Ross, Barney, 99, 122

Saddler, Sandy, 34, 90, 99, 160-161, 162
   illus., 163-164
Sánchez, Salvador, 66
Schmeling, Max, 121
Sharkey, Jack, 22
Shavers, Earnie, 69-70, 152-154, 153 *illus.*, 171
Silvani, Al (trainer), 33
Smith, Buck, 73
Spinks, Leon, 20, 21, 46, 128 *illus.*, 129-134, 135 *illus.*, 136-137
   defeats Muhammad Ali, 103, 129, 131-132
Spinks, Michael, 21, 32, 34, 46, 130 *illus.*, 136, 137, 171
   defeats Larry Holmes, 69
   knocked out by Mike Tyson, 100, 103
   relationship with brother Leon, 129-131
   in retirement, 126
   titles held, 80
sportswriters, 77
Steward, Emanuel (trainer), 31, 35, 59, 126
Stillman, Lou (gym owner), 33
Stillman's Gym (New York), 33-34, 99
Sullivan, John L., 122

Tate, John, 20, 122
television, effect on boxing, 76-77, 90
Terranova, Phil, 34